The Bronx is Burning

A novel by

Al Efron, FAIA

The Bronx is Burning

Copyright © 2019

by

Al Efron, FAIA

Printed in the United States of America

Tucson, Arizona

Other Novels by Al Efron, FAIA:

- Never Tell Me, "You Can't Do That" My Life's Journey
- Guilty Until Proven Innocent
- Hourglass Lake
- Faces of the World (Photography book)
- Greed & Murder
- The Big Bank Scam
- The Toothless Diamond
- The Cigarette Explosion

Authors Note:

This book is part nonfiction biography and part novel of the South Bronx. The nonfiction biography portion begins with chapter 1 and continues to chapter 4 page 5. At this point, this book becomes a novel.

The South Bronx is a portion of the borough of the Bronx. The borough of the Bronx is one borough of the five boroughs that makes up "New York City ".

Chapter 1

A Quick Biography

This book will cover the years of 1950, 1960, 1970, and a portion of 1980 and 1990.

The South Bronx is divided into four mainly unique communities named Concourse, Mott Haven, Melrose, and Port Morris. There are some other minor communities that are also considered part of the South Bronx.

The South Bronx is noted for the creation of hip-hop and the art of graffiti.

After World War II, new housing was built to accommodate the returning servicemen.

Due to slum clearance in the borough of Manhattan, mostly Black's and Puerto Rican's relocated to the South Bronx.

In order to prevent the skyrocketing of rents due to the lack of adequate housing, the New York City government created rent control. Rent control made provisions for finical support for any tenant as well as the landlords who were burned out of their apartment or lost the building to fire. After a while, some of the unscrupulous landlords would set fire to their buildings as well as the tenants setting fire to their apartments to take advantage of all the regulations and insurance that were part of rent control. These fires burned buildings located at one end of the block to the other end of the block, burning every building along the way. In addition, fires were started to as many buildings in the area that they were able to set on fire. The tenants of burned out buildings or apartments were given financing and priority to move into new public housing. These fires started in the 1960s and continued into the early 1970s. The self-made fires stopped when the regulations were changed to limit the advantage of being burned out of your home.

Because of the huge number of these fires that were continually burning a large portion of the South Bronx, the phrase, "The Bronx is burning", became popular.

After a very long period of destruction, government was finally able to start the reconstruction of the South Bronx by building new one family homes, many row houses, apartment buildings as well as the restoration where possible of existing building. This construction created hundreds of new apartments. Many apartments were converted to cooperatives and condominium units allowing residents of the South Bronx to own their own home.

In time the population changed when a growing number of Koreans, Indian, Pakistani, Cubans, Dominicans, Jamaicans, Greek, Russians, and Albanians settled in the South Bronx.

At the beginning of the 1990s, due to the huge urban renewal of the South Bronx, the National Civic Council awarded the South Bronx the title of "All American City".

Chapter 2

The Presidential Candidate Arrives

At the height of the South Bronx disaster in the 1970s, entire blocks were on fire, many burned out or vandalized. Broken and burned automobiles were evident on every street. Fire hydrants were destroyed as the water was gushing out, and residents of all ages were strolling around going nowhere and were living nowhere because of this mass self-destruction of the entire area.

The year was 1977, at the height of the presidential campaign. Democratic candidate, a State Senator as well as past Governor of the state of Georgia, was campaigning to become the 39th President of the United States. James Earl Carter Junior, better known as Jimmy Carter, made a campaign stop in the heart of the South Bronx. He stood there not believing what he was seeing. How can a community come in the state of such destruction with no signs of trying to get control? Because of this situation, he reasoned, government should be creating new required housing for all those people that were just strolling around or sitting at the curb with no place to go and nothing to do. This situation was so far from the imagination of candidate Carter, who was a peanut farmer in the state of Georgia. He never experienced such destruction and hopelessness as he was seeing that day.

The group of local politicians that were escorting the candidate around the area, explained the political problems, lack of funds and lack of leadership that was preventing the rebuilding of this entire neighborhood. This situation cannot be handled locally because of the huge size of the area and money required. The United States Federal Government must get involved.

After Carter completed a thorough in-depth briefing and seeing the situation for himself as he was walking and trying not to get too close to all those fires still burning on every street, he faced the delegation of local politicians and stated, "If, or should I say, when I become president of the United States, the situation that I see today will get my full attention and I will do whatever I can to make this community a great place to live in."

All the New York City newspapers ran the headlines describing the presidential candidate and his trip through the destruction of the South Bronx. Everyone was feeling some hope that if he gets elected and becomes our president and remembers what he saw today, he will live up to his promise and take action.

In the middle of the 1970s, Ronald Reagan also visited the area. As a result of the Jimmy Carter and Ronald Reagan visit, money started the flow through the United States Department of Housing and Urban Development, better known as HUD. Reconstruction was on its way.

At this time, it was standard procedure when government is allocating money to be spent on a particular project, some form of government was involved and responsible to make sure that all the money shall be legally spent for the intended project.

In reviewing this particular formula for spending the money with government control, they found that it did not work out as intended. In so many cases, the money made its way through stealing and/or a variety of other illegal forms of spending the money and in the illegal pockets of a variety of a number of the wrong government people.

To ensure that all the money shall be spent on the project as intended, the money for rebuilding the South Bronx shall be given to a neighborhood legally set up nonprofit organization. This nonprofit organization shall consist of individuals that are living in the reconstruction area. The feeling was that if the money is given to the people that actually live in the area, then all the money will be spent for building the project to be used by themselves as residents living in the area and will benefit the entire new reconstructed community.

Chapter 3

Time to Rebuild our Homes

The new Board of Directors and members of the local nonprofit organization were now fully organized and ready to start the building process.

The first order of business was to take stock of the entire area. Once that is complete, they can then work up a plan to replace all the property that was burned out or are in a dangerous condition at the present time.

Task number one was to interview architects and higher the architect with the knowledge and office capability of handling a project of this size.

The nonprofit board created a list of architects that were qualified to design the entire area and prepare a demolition drawing for removal of all structures that are not to be part of this final project. A letter was sent to all the qualified architects to submit an RFP, "Request for proposal".

Once all RFP's were received by the nonprofit board, interviews were arranged. All the approved architects were given a date and time for their interview. A meeting was now set up between the nonprofit board and the proposed architect. The architect was notified of the time and date established for his, or her presentation.

After a week of deliberation by the nonprofit board, they selected three architects that they felt were qualified to handle this project. The board then set up interviews with the architect that was number one on the list. If for any reason they could not hire that architect, then they went to architect number two of the list. They followed this procedure until a contract was signed, hiring that architect.

At the time of the meeting, members of the nonprofit board met in the first architect's office. The chairman of the Board of Directors did the introductions. He started by saying, "My name is James Sullivan and I am chairman of the board. Sitting next to me is Carl Webster. He is vice chairman of the board. Sitting next to Carl is Mariano Messina. He is treasurer of the board. Finally, the secretary of the board is Fred Berman." At that point, the architect introduced himself by saying, "As you know, my name is Al Benjamin. Next to me is my partner Peter Barron." The discussion of the project got underway covering all facets of this project, how they would be handled, and all the other problems and solutions of a project of this size and nature. The architect said at one point that his office did a number of similar projects and are familiar with all the requirements to produce a perfect successful project.

About an hour of discussing the problems and solutions of the project, one of the board members stated to the architect, "I assume that you realize that the four of us are the complete Board of Directors. There is no one we must answer to and have full authority and control over the entire building process of this community. Therefore, I suppose you know you will have to have our people on your unofficial staff." "Yes", the architect stated. "Your person on my staff gives us the ability to share information with your people. We would be able to have close coordination between my office and the Board of Directors. We avoid a lot of misunderstanding by having someone from your organization on my staff to keep the board up-to-date as the project proceeds."

The chairman of the board then said, "Do you mean our person on our staff will be a staff member like the rest of your employees?" "Yes, of course", the architect said. "My accountant will be reporting to all federal authorities the same way my accountant does for the rest of my staff. Everything will be documented and 100% legal."

"I guess you don't understand", said the chairman. "You would have to pay our people, the exact number of people I do not know yet, on your staff cash and nothing can be reported to anyone. We will tell you the amount of the money that you pay our employees once we get everything settled. You know, we have quite a few people that have to get a piece of that action."

The architect looked at his partner and they both couldn't believe what they were hearing. "I'm sorry, the architect said, we do not do business that way. Everything would have to be completely legal." "Well then, the chairman said, we will not be able to hire you as our architect." "I guess if that's the case, the architect said, thank you for considering us and I wish you all the luck on your new project." At that point, the members of the nonprofit board left the office as the architect and his partner just stood there not believing what just happened in this conference room.

This meeting between the nonprofit board and the proposed architect is 100% fact. I, the author of this book, was the architect selected by the board to be the architect for the entire project. Therefore, I was present at this meeting.

At the conclusion of this meeting, I looked at my partner with an expression of disbelief of what just happened. My partner agreed with me by turning down their offer. I was not sure if they were wired and recording this meeting for some prosecutor trying to flush out all the architects that take and give bribes, or just a group of crooks trying to make a lot of money.

An unhappy reminder,

The government felt that if the community handled the money they would be honest and not be involved in any graft or illegal pay off or any other illegal operation. All the money would go towards construction of their homes. How wrong they were. It doesn't matter if you work for the government or work for yourself, there are always those unscrupulous people and organizations.

And now I start the Novel

Chapter 4

Getting the Architect on Board

It did not take long for the Board of Directors to find an architect whose ethics agree with the type of ethics and construction of the Board of Directors. It did not matter if the architect is not familiar with this type of project and never handled a project of this construction type and size, as long as the architect is willing to play it the boards way. The architect just hopes to enjoy the dirty money that he or she will be getting.

The architectural firm of, Benjamin and Baron, was the architect that the Board of Directors hired. This architectural firm is a small organization consisting of the two architectural partners, five draftsman plus one secretary. Most of this architects work and experience was dealing with one family home developers who build large tract cookie-cutter type buildings. The architect for this type of construction prepares simple non-detailed drawings of four different design types of one family homes. There is always just enough information on each drawing to obtain an approval from the Building Department. Once the architect gives the developer the approved drawings and related paperwork, the developer starts building the way he or she want to, and the architect has no further involvement in this project.

In rebuilding the South Bronx, when construction was completed, the tenants and apartment owners start moving into these new buildings. That's when the trouble starts. The mechanical systems does not work efficiently due to the shortcuts that was taken during construction, plus a huge amount of other minor and major problems including cracks and leaks in the basement walls allowing water to flood the entire basement. Noise can be heard between apartments for lack of soundproofing, and many other problems start popping up all over the project. Because of all these problems, the contractor and Board of Directors were able to walk away with quite a large sum of money.

The sad fact of life is that when a situation like this occurs, the building contractor who's responsible to take care of all the problems that keep popping up, is not available because, one, they now have all their money, two, they go out of business, and three, they then reorganize under another name so they are not responsible for any problems of that project. The contract is then with a new legal name and starts the same process at another development. BUYER BEWHERE!!!

The architect in starting this project, set up a meeting with the New York City Traffic Department and Building Departments to obtain all the information on regulations for laying out the entire street and traffic pattern, plus lot sizes for each building type to make sure that the final product conforms with all required laws and regulations require to obtain the approval of all government agencies. The architect as a courtesy stated that when he has a complete site plan he will issue a copy for comments to the Traffic Department and Building Department. The next chore that the architect requires is a meeting with the Board of Directors to establish a construction schedule. Projects like commercial garages and retail stores to service the local residents?

Once the architect obtained all the information needed, a complete site plan of this project will be created for approval of the new South Bronx.

At this time in the creation of a new South Bronx, the Board of Directors was inundated with requests to buy or rent apartments and or retail space. When the construction is completed, moving into the apartments as well as various retail spaces that will service this new area will begin. Because of all these inquiries, the Board of Directors set up an office type temporary trailer with trained staff on the site to properly handle the requests. The staff would be able to create contracts and start the renting or selling apartments, one family homes, as well as establish commercial areas as part of the development to service all the local residents.

It was now time for the Board of Directors to start an in depth study of the entire area to be conducted to ensure that the architect is directed to include all the nonresidential areas on this site in a proper location.

A meeting with the Board of Directors, the architect, and a New York City official, who is familiar with this type of development, called the meeting to make sure that all the ancillary facilities are included in this project.

The meeting was scheduled for the following Monday morning and all the invited personnel were notified of the meeting. On the Monday morning of the meeting, everyone was in attendance as they were seated at the conference table with the standard cup of coffee and snack. The coffee and snack is vital to ensure that everyone would have the energy and stay awake at this entire important meeting.

The first person to speak was the New York City official. He quickly outlined some of the ancillary facilities that should be included in this project. The first item was that some single family homes must be included. In addition, there should be enough space for a shopping center with ample parking large enough to service all of the residents of this community. Lastly, a park or some other type of open space for the enjoyment of all the residents of this area. It would be nice, but not really necessary, to provide a lake or waterway around the perimeter of the park that can be used by rowboats and kayaks. In addition, every effort must be made so that police and fire department personnel have full and easy access to the entire area when needed.

The architect then stated that all these requirements are fine and can definitely recommend to include them in the design of the area. "However, I recommend that in the park we should not put that waterway around the entire park. That has a very expensive construction costs as well maintenance. There is the need for several full time staff to manage that waterway. It must be kept clean so no growth can start sprouting up at the bottom. There has to be monitoring for any leaks that may occur due to expansion and contraction with the changes of temperature at the various times of the year. There should also be a full time attendant on hand in case of anyone falling into that waterway or having their kayak, rowboats or anything else that is on this waterway capsize and is needed to be rescued."

The chairman of the board quickly stated that the lake or waterway around the park should not be built. Then continued, "It will not be built. Everything else that was put on the table by our New York City representative should be positively included in this project if it makes economic sense."

After much discussion, they broke for lunch. When everyone returned from their afternoon meal the chairman of the board stated, "Taking into consideration everything that was mentioned this morning makes sense and should be included in the project. We shall provide some single family homes, some garden apartments, a park without any waterway, and a shopping center. All of these units shall be of the proper size to service this new community." The chairman also stated, "I would like to enter one more small item, and that would be a management facility containing an office for the manager, a conference room, a file room, a storage room, adequate toilet facilities, small kitchenette providing coffee etc. for meetings as well as light lunches for the staff when required."

After about another hour of open discussion, it was agreed to put all required items in a memo that will be signed by all members at this meeting and issued to the architect to include in his plans.

Everyone agreed and the document was created, signed and distributed. The meeting ended and all the attendees left for the day. The architect, in designing the site plan, indicating that the majority of the housing in this development shall be six-story elevated apartments. In addition, he provided twenty four, two story garden apartments as well as an area containing twenty one single family homes. A park will be located in the center of the entire development with a shopping center across the street from the park that will have easy access for the entire residents of this community. In addition, he created a project management office, as outlined in the memo, that was located in the shopping center.

To satisfy the parking requirements of this project, the architect provided parking at the lower level below the first floor of all the six story elevated buildings solely for the use of the occupants of each building, on site off street parking for the garden apartments and an area for parking for each individual single family home at the front yard up against the side lot line.

When the architect completed the entire site plan, he submitted plans to the Board of Directors for comments. He also submitted copies to the Traffic Department and Building Department as previously agreed to by all parties. In addition, as a courtesy, copies of the drawings be submitted to the Fire Department and Police Department for their comments.

After a period of time, all parties receiving copies of the site plan and had ample time to study its contents, a meeting was scheduled for attendance by all parties to ensure that the final product satisfies the requirements of all departments.

As a result of that major meeting by all parties, the architect was given a number of corrections and revisions that have to be made for final approval. It took the architect two weeks to complete all the requests and suggestions by all the departments and resubmitted, with hope this was the final site plan.

Three weeks went by when the architect received the approval of his drawings by all parties. Now the architect went to work creating the final construction documents that all construction companies will use to build this entire new community. The architect and his engineers completed the construction drawings for their design of the individual buildings and ancillary facilities that included all the designs for the structural parts of the building, heating and air conditioning, plumbing, electrical, and landscaping. Once all designs were complete, they were issued to the Building Department for approval. After a number of adjustments to the drawings that the Building Department required, the architect received the final approval of his drawings so that construction can begin. This project is now "A GO".

Chapter 5

Beginning the Coordinating of Construction Phase

At this point all the construction contractors and members of the Board of Directors held a private, secret meeting to go over the drawings and specifications to find areas that they can make small adjustments to the drawings as well as using less expensive equipment to replace the expensive required equipment that the architect and engineers noted in their specifications and drawings. The contractors and Board of Directors felt confident that no one will ever suspect that they made minor changes as well as using cheaper equipment substitutions. All these changes and substitutions will produce a large amount of money that will end up in all the board members and construction companies' pockets.

The list of adjusted items contained a huge variety of all the heating and ventilating, electrical, plumbing equipment as well as general construction equipment such as kitchen and bathroom equipment and facilities etc. Listing of the high quality equipment specified turned out to be low quality equipment being installed.

This system will continue through every phase of the construction of this entire project. When you start adding up the money being saved that will be going into the pockets of the Board of Directors and construction companies, the total amount is huge. And then in the near future when things start falling apart, those contractors will be paid to fix or replace the items that cease to work anymore. So the contractors are getting paid to fix what they got paid for that created the problem.

The first order of normal business was to start the process of repairing and creating new sidewalks and roadways within the entire project area. All the new utilities from each building has to be coordinated with the various city agencies so that all the existing sewers, water piping, electrical can properly receive and connect to each other. The architect and his engineers work closely with the cities engineers to make sure all utilities will be working properly and totally coordinated to receive the new community's utilities.

The next order of business was to lay out all the property lines so that each new building will be built on a legal lot.

The architect and his engineers that work very closely with all the city agencies involved to make sure that this new community is properly served and coordinated with the rest of the city.

The architect and his engineers prepared all the documents as required and filed them with the city for their comments, approval, or any changes that the various New York City agencies require.

There were many meetings with the architect, his engineers, and the engineers from the city. These lengthy meetings were to discuss all the additional details that have to be carefully worked out. The architect and his engineers then submitted their adjusted drawings for approval to the city agencies. If the cities engineers require additional changes, they have to be made and resubmitted to the city agencies again. If any additional comments were made, the drawings again had to be prepared and resubmitted again to the city until final approval is received.

Finally, all the necessary drawings or approved by the contractor had the green light to start creating the new city.

All the paperwork and coordination between the contractors and all the city agencies were now in place. Inspectors from the Building Department and other city agencies had their inspection schedules all set. The creation of a new community was now in motion.

Chapter 6

Construction Started

One of the construction companies group of surveyors started to lay out all the new streets and sidewalks in conjunction with the existing streets and sidewalks as approved by the city of New York.

The second construction companies group of surveyors started to layout each individual lot in size and location to satisfy the type of building that will be constructed on each site in conformance with the New York City zoning code.

While the two surveying groups were busy doing their work, the rest of the construction crews were gearing up to start the excavation and installing foundations.

While all this preliminary work that was going on with the surveyors, a young man named William Morris Thompson lives very close to this new community that was being built in the South Bronx. This young man just graduated from the College of Cooper Union with the degree in architecture. This new graduate with his degree in architecture did not as yet seek out employment. He felt he needed some personal time after the long five years of studying architecture. With this degree, the young man will have to have three years of practical experience working for an architect in order to become eligible to take the state board exams and obtain his license to practice architecture. He reasoned that it would be beneficial for him to spend some time observing construction as it is progressing in real time before he takes a job working for an architect to get his three years of practical experience. It would be very interesting to see how different construction is in the field versus the college experience.

The next day, he parked his car right next to an empty lot across the street from the construction site. He took a folding web type beach chair from the back of his car and set it up on the empty lot. He then sat down, took out a thermos that contained fresh hot coffee, and started to observe the construction. By the third day, one of the construction worker, who happened to be a foreman, noticed this young man sitting across the street and watching what was going on all day long. Out of pure curiosity the foreman approached the young man, introduced himself and asked if he was enjoying the view. William then told the foreman that he just received his degree in architecture and felt it would be beneficial to him if he watched to see how construction works in real life.

The foreman sees this bright young man making a true effort to learn the practical end of the construction phase of the building industry so he could compare it with his formal school education. The foreman then said, "My name is Angelo Matero. I am the foreman of this construction team. You seem to have what looks like working clothing. Come with me and we will give you a good education right up front during the construction. You will be an unpaid member of my crew that does not have to work. You just have to watch and ask questions. I have a form that we have all individuals' sign that are visiting the site and are not part of the construction team. All this form says is that you hold us harmless if you have an accident, or get hurt on the construction site. It is just a formality that we have for anyone visiting the site to protect both parties. How does that sound?" "Great, said William, let me put my chair in the car." Once the chair was put away, Williams said to his new friend, the foreman, "Give me the form for me to sign and then I will look like a real construction worker."

It did not take long for William to feel that he was part of the construction team. William started soaking up all the knowledge and information that he observed and was also told by his new friends.

The construction day passed very quickly for William. He was loving every minute of on-the-job of a real construction project. Not only was he able to observe and experience the actual construction work, he was also able to compare the construction with the architectural drawings that makes the entire process possible.

William arrived at the construction site every morning before the rest of the crew arrived. He was anxious to get started with another great day of learning by actual observing and from time to time doing the actual work of creating a building. He was very studious, checking the architectural drawings and comparing it with the completed work of that portion of the building. William then started to realize that a large number of the specified components on the architectural drawings were not built into the building as required. What was built into the project was a much cheaper, inferior substitute product. This substitution would never be as efficient as the item specified and would not last near the life of the specified item. He asked the foreman if he was reading the drawings correctly as he compared them with the actual construction. The foreman then stated that he uses "poetic license" interpreting the architectural drawings that is a somewhat acceptable unwritten policy in the construction industry. That statement started William thinking, that was a weird answer that just didn't seem correct. William now started to check the architectural drawings very carefully and comparing them not only with the actual construction but also with the equipment that was being installed in the kitchens and bathrooms as well as other equipment such as components of the heating and air conditioning equipment being installed. It became quite obvious to William that this construction crew was building a final product that was not only supplying cheaper equipment from what was specified but also inferior final construction than what was called for on the architectural drawings.

William was concerned with what he was learning and started taking notes documenting all the conditions that he felt was being constructed or installed in the building that did not comply with the approved architectural drawings. Williams's notes of all these conditions was growing into a book.

That night after dinner, William was thinking of the situation he was in with that growing book documenting the inferior construction conditions. The foreman and all the construction workers were so nice to him that he felt like they were his friends and he was their friend. If for some unforeseen condition that I am documenting of what I found out that was going on during construction goes public, I will be hurting all those new friends that I was working with on the construction site.

He then came to the conclusion that he should stop working on the construction site. He will tell his friends that he is getting a job with the architect to put in his required three years of practical experience in preparation for qualifying him to take the state board exam. Once he becomes a licensed architect, he will then decide what to do with that document he created while working on the construction site.

Chapter 7

Draftsman to Architect

It did not take long for William to obtain employment working for a large architectural firm in the position of a new employee junior draftsman. This architectural firm had 200 employees and specialized in building new hospitals, nursing homes, and other facilities in the healthcare field worldwide. The advantage of working for a large firm is that there was always the possibility of advancement to becoming a project leader which meant receiving a large salary advancement. This position is in charge of a team of draftsman and various engineers to produce all the required drawings and documents for the bidding process to obtain the construction companies that will be building this facility.

William started his new position with built-up energy to do the best job he can and learn the practical side of creating architectural and engineering documents that will be actually used for construction.

Always in the back of William's mind was his notes of that South Bronx construction company that might be proceeding with construction that was not legal.

The three years that William was working to obtain the requirement to take the state board exam, went quickly. He now sent in his application to take the state board exams on his road of coming a practicing architect. The exam consisted of seven individual parts covering all aspects of the architectural profession. It took four separate days to complete all seven parts of the exam. In order to obtain your license to practice architecture you must pass all seven parts. This is one of the most difficult exams that William ever faced while going through college.

After completing the exam William had a long wait for the state board to examine all the exams from every applicant before making the announcement of all those students who passed their exam.

Finally, William received an official letter notifying him that he passed the exam and was now legally able to start the practice of an architect.

William, was now a very bright, hardworking, licensed architect. In the three years that he worked as a draftsman, his boss, the senior partner of the firm, took notice of this young intelligent draftsman who now was a licensed architect. He was offered the position of junior partner to the firm. William quickly accepted the offer and was now on the road to great success as a practicing architect.

However, those notes that he wrote from the South Bronx construction was still and always on his mind.

Chapter 8

The Project Goes Public

Just about four years has passed since William was the volunteer worker of rebuilding of the South Bronx. William is now a licensed architect and junior partner in a large architectural firm located in Manhattan. William's office is about a twenty minute drive from his office, depending on the traffic conditions, to the South Bronx construction area. William could not resist the opportunity to revisit his friends working on that construction site. One bright sunny afternoon, he took the time and drove down to the South Bronx to visit his construction friends and see how the construction was progressing.

When the construction workers noticed William approaching the building, they yelled out to him with a warm welcome back and excited gestures. It was a great new reunion of the friendship that has developed between William and his fellow construction workers.

Construction of this new community has reached approximately 40% completed. The entire area that was completed was now occupied by tenants living in the new apartments and the various retail stores in the area were doing a brisk business.

Everyone now calmed down and started the conversation to update one another with the latest developments in their individual lives. Construction workers were delighted to learn that William was now a registered architect and junior partner in a large architectural firm. They all shouted out, "Local boy makes good." William then started the conversation in reference to the construction that has been completed and now occupied. He asked how the buildings that are now occupied standing up. The Foreman then answer the question by saying, "The truth is that we are not very happy with the results of our labor. When we were hired to do all the construction we had to agree to make all and every change from the details noted on the architectural drawings as directed by the Board of Directors of the nonprofit organization. There construction company boss and the chairman of the Board of Directors made it very clear to us that if we do not comply with his changes we will no longer be working on this project."

"The maintenance of the buildings requires a large staff of workers to keep the buildings and apartments in good condition. We are sorry to say that we are not very proud of our work due to the final substitution of equipment and adjusted constructed conditions. If we wanted to work, we had no choice but to comply with our boss and the chairman of the Board of Directors."

William then confided in his working friends that he noticed all the changes that were made of the conditions noted on the architectural drawings and specifications. In fact William continued, "I kept a diary of all the changes that were finally made. My diary is my secret and no one at this time has seen what I noted."

"The big question now is what do we do with the information of the inferior conditions of the construction and the substitution of equipment that the not so honorable directions that we were given by the Board of Directors? Do we just accept the fact that the substandard construction is causing all that excessive maintenance, or do we go public with this information?"

Foreman then burst out saying, "I have the solution. If we can get William hired by the Board of Directors as the architect to provide all the necessary drawings and Building Department approvals of all the corrective work that has to be done throughout the entire project, then the money saved due to the deliberate poor construction that ended up in the pockets of the Board of Directors will be spent on the corrected work instead of back charging all the tenants. This information can then slowly be leaked out to the government authorities."

"Wait a minute", the Foreman said. "I think I have a better solution. Just this morning we noticed that the heavy beam supporting the large multipurpose community room and auditorium that was installed instead of that special designed expensive truss, was showing very small signs of weakening. We noticed very slight cracks develop around the walls. We were going to notify the engineers to check out that possible dangerous condition. Since that building has not yet been occupied there was no danger to any occupants of the building as yet. Maybe we should wait and let nature take its course. As the beam continues to weaken, larger cracks will develop and the condition will look dangerous enough for photographers to photograph that condition for the daily newspaper. Then the illegal operation of the Board of Directors will become public. The engineers then will come up with the corrective work to prevent that area from collapsing."

"Great idea. Let's check out that situation again right now to make sure that there would be no danger of collapse until the situation goes public." This small troop of plotters then very closely examined the entire area all around that portion of the building. The Foreman then said, "I feel very comfortable with the fact that this condition at this moment is not dangerous.

Let's watch this condition very closely until it looks dangerous, and is ready to collapse at that time. Then we contact our engineers and leak the information to the newspapers."

Our band of plotters were very carefully monitoring the structural condition every few hours. It took about four days before they noticed some major cracking in the walls. The Foreman then pronounced, "It is time to go into action."

They quickly notify the engineers that they discovered a dangerous condition that needs their attention immediately. Within an hour the engineers appeared at the site and started their in-depth investigation. The first thing they noticed was a large structural member holding up the entire area was not what was specified by the designing engineers. The structural member that was installed definitely does not have the capacity to support that large span. They immediately ordered structural supports to be jacked up under the existing beam to prevent any failure. They then contacted the architect so they can coordinate the necessary corrective method of removing that failing structural unit and replacing it with the proper truss and rebuilding the entire area around this condition. As the engineers and the architect were discussing the situation, lo and behold a photographer and reporter from the local newspaper just happened to be on the site at that time. The photographer's flashgun kept popping off as he was taking photographs, illustrating the horrible dangerous construction. The next day's edition of the local newspaper had a major story on the front cover with a number of photographs to document the terrible dangerous condition. The Mayor then instructed the District Attorney to conduct an entire investigation into this situation as well as any other possible dangerous conditions that might have been built into the project illegally. Since there was federal money in this project, the FBI also sent two agents down to assess the situation.

Chapter 9

The Investigation

The District Attorney contacted the architect William Morris Thompson, AIA and appoint him to serve on an investigating committee. He also asked the architect to recommending other professionals in the construction industry for positions on this committee. The architect agreed to serve and recommended a number of good engineering that he worked with on other projects. The architect William Morris Thompson, AIA plus a number of engineers that he worked with over the years and had the confidence that they will do an in-depth investigation.

Lester White, one of the FBI agents, also contacted the architect William and coordinated their efforts with what the investigating committee would be finding.

After reading the daily newspaper, the Chairman of the Board called an emergency meeting to discuss the proper way to handle the situation with minimum impact.

All the board members were now seated around the conference table. The eyes of every board member were focused on the chairman. Just looking at their eyes you can see that they expressed deep worry. "How did a situation like this go public so fast? We had this entire project under control until the situation popped up. We have to make sure that the only item that goes public from now on is this one incident. We have to sell the idea that the rest of the project is safe and completely livable. I suggest that we hire a public relations firm to start getting some articles out to the public to downplay this one incident." The chairman then said, "Is everyone in agreement to hire a public relations firm?" The result was a unanimous yes.

The chairman then continued, "From now on, no one is authorized to have any interviews, or speak to any and all media people. I will be the only spokesman to speak on behalf of the entire project. I will accept any of your thoughts and comments for my consideration in presenting our side of this incident. All agreed?" Another unanimous yes.

The chairman then continued, "Don't worry, I will have the situation under control in no time at all. No one will ever know of all the substitutions that we made so that we can save on the construction and pocket the excess money. So just stop worrying and keep your mouth shut. This meeting is now adjourned."

The board members started to leave the room with a worried look on their faces as they turned away from the chairman and left the room. One of the members was heard saying in a low voice, "I hope the chairman knows what he's doing?"

In the meantime, the investigating committee was formed and was ready to look into every aspect of the construction as it compares with all the architectural and engineering drawings and details that was approved by the Building Department for construction.

An Assistant District Attorney was appointed as chairman of the committee, and also coordinated their findings with the FBI agents.

The first meeting was held and started to organize the procedure that they will follow. They divided the group into four inspection teams. Each team represented a specific area of construction.

Team number one, architectural, was headed by the architect William Morris Thompson, AIA.

Team number two, heating ventilating and air conditioning, was headed by the engineer Ralph Summers, PE.

Team number three, electrical, was headed by Seymour Cohen, PE.

Team number four, plumbing, was headed by Alfred Simonton, PE.

There were four additional professional engineers and architects that were assigned to the various teams within their specialty.

The total size of the total teams equal 20 professional engineers and architects.

All the teams agreed that only one team at a time will be in an area of inspection.

Each team was given a full set of Building Department approved architectural and engineering drawings and specifications for their specific specialty. In addition, they were given a copy of all the notes that indicated substitutions and redesign areas compiled by architect William Morris Thompson when he was a volunteer working on the site.

Each team organized themselves and started going through all of the completed construction that was still vacant, as well as occupied to compare the actual construction with the proved Building Department approved drawings.

Those locations that were occupied by either a business on the street level or a family in the upper apartments were notified of the inspections and were requested to give the inspection team complete access to their areas.

It did not take long for all the teams to realize that all the problems in similar buildings were exactly the same. So to save time they divided the entire area to the different types of buildings and selected one of each type for inspection. During their inspections, if anything seemed that it might be different in another building of the same type, then they would check out the other building.

Four weeks went by and a meeting was held for each committee to report their findings so far. The head of each committee then gave the report of what they found. The results of all the committees were mind blowing. The list of changing details and material or equipment was huge. The head of each committee put down their written report that look like one of those huge dictionaries that you see on a stand in the library.

To try to ascertain the amount of money that was saved by all those changes and substitutions will take a team of estimators a number of weeks. The big problem that each team encountered was that the substituted construction that was used was inferior and needed quite a bit of maintenance to keep them running properly. Therefore, it was assumed that the saved money the management pocketed was not keeping all those conditions up to date. In speaking with the occupants of those apartments or stores, there were many complaints that most of the maintenance problems were never fixed the date they spoke to the management. They were told that it's on the books and will be fixed shortly. However, shortly never came.

Finally, when all the inspections were completed, a huge report was submitted to the authorities finalizing this portion of the work.

The District Attorney and the FBI, coordinating their efforts, to ascertain where all the money that was saved because of these changes went, who was responsible for making these changes, were there dangerous conditions that might fail, were there illegal procedures by management of this construction, and finally, who do we prosecute.

The FBI and the District Attorney agreed that all the legal work and prosecutions will be done by the District Attorney with input and coordination with the FBI.

Chapter 10

Looking for the Bad Guys

The first group of individuals that the District Attorney had his eyes on were the designing architect and engineers whose contract had a clause that they will do "periodic observations" during the entire construction process. Periodic observation is a requirement that the American Institute of Architects puts in there standard AIA contracts. The vast amount of architects use that contract. Periodic observation means that the architect and/or engineers shall conduct site visits and observe, not supervise, the construction conditions to make sure they are keeping with the approved drawings. There was absolutely no records found indicating that the architect and engineers complied with this portion of their contract.

The second group was the Board of Directors. The government put together this Board of Directors by selecting all the members and chairmen who were current residents living in the construction area. The Board of Directors then entered into contracts with a design team consisting of the architect and engineers that will design the entire project. The contract between the government and the board stated that the Board of Directors shall conduct competitive bidding from construction companies, award construction contracts to the winning construction company. The board shall manage the entire project. The government will provide the money to the Board of Directors who shall manage the money to pay all bills required as part of the construction process.

The District Attorney's staff started to investigate the flow of money that was paid by the government to the Board of

Directors that ended up illegally with each board member. In tracing the money to each individual director, they discovered that a small amount of money was the payment part of their legal compensation for serving on the board.

After fully checking the flow of money entering each Board of Directors accounts, they were able to trace a large amount of the money flowing into each director's account that was received from the government and designated for payment to the construction companies.

The investigators also discovered a large amount of money flowing into personal accounts of the chairman of the board plus all the board members from various suppliers of construction material.

The money flowing illegally from the construction to the personal accounts of members of the Board of Directors was growing into very large numbers.

The investigators continued their search and were able to find documentation from the Board of Directors that directed the construction companies to install substitute items of construction in place of the official specified material. The difference in cost from the expensive specified material to the installed substitute items was then paid to the Board of Directors. This money was then divided up so each director received their share of this money. The investigators then were able to trace the money to the individual director's bank accounts.

As the investigators kept digging into all the records at their disposal, the theft and corruption kept showing up and the money involved kept flowing to the entire Board of Directors bank accounts.

The investigators also found records indicating that the architect and engineers who worked on this project also received some of that illegally acquired money.

To sum up this situation in a few words it meant that, "The Board of Directors got richer and the construction got pourer."

The investigators then started to examine all the records in a number of additional files cabinets that were discovered in the closet of the Board of Directors office. These files indicated a huge amount of documents that were submitted to the insurance companies to cover the cost of accidents, theft, and other insurable conditions on the construction site. The grand total came to a little over $200,000. Again, checking the bank records the investigators were able to trace the money from the insurance companies directly to the members of the Board of Directors.

This insurance fraud raise questions with the investigators as to the procedure followed with the filing of each insurance claim. After the investigation and interrogation of the insurance agents and claims adjusters, they found more dishonest involvement, plus the added amount of money. It seems that the insurance adjusters got, as they say, a piece of the action.

With every new development and action found in every section of this construction project, money was flowing into the individual pockets of the people without any scruples.

The replacement of a burned-out community was a very inferior construction of a new city.

Chapter 11

The Trial Begins

The Judge assigned to this case is Harold Fitzpatrick. The Assistant District Attorney assigned to prosecute this case is Nancy Halloway.

The investigators found documentation that the designing architect and engineers were part of this free flowing of money. It was now quite clear why the architect and engineers did not conduct periodic observations. This evidence, plus all the documentation that the investigators discovered while tracing the flow of money, can prove that the chairman and board members of the nonprofit organization were each receiving a large amount of the money that was supposed to be dedicated for construction. In addition, the investigators found that the insurance adjusters were also on the receiving end of this money.

At this point, the Assistant District Attorney started to put her case together for the prosecution of all the members of the Board of Directors, plus the chairman, as well as the architect and all the design engineers and insurance adjusters who will be charged with various crimes and prosecuted the full extent of the law.

The first legal course of action to be taken by the prosecuting attorney will be against the chairman of the board including all the board members. They were charged with grand theft and endangering the lives of all the residents and businesses that occupied apartments and stores as well as all people part of the general public in the vicinity of each substandard buildings or stores that was part of the construction.

The Judge then looked at the attorney for the accused and for the government and stated we will now proceed with the jury selection.

Each potential juror was then brought before the court for questioning by the attorneys for the accused and the defense. Attorneys from each side of this case then asked the usual questions to ascertain whatever information they needed to either accept that person to serve on the jury or to be dismissed.

At the conclusion of this process, a jury was assembled and the Judge went through the legal procedures. At the conclusion of the Judge's remarks to the jury, they were seated in their designated area.

At this time, the Judge asked the chairman and each board member how they plea. The chairman pleaded not guilty, and then each board member in turn pleaded not guilty except for the last board member standing in front of the Judge with his head down looking at his feet as he said in a low voice, "Guilty Your Honor." At that point, you can hear the shock wave that went to the bodies of the chairman of the board and all other board members who pleaded not guilty. There was also a whisper that went through all the visitors that attended this trial. The Judge then looked at this last board member and asked him if he would please repeat his plea to make sure there's no misunderstanding. Still standing with his head down looking at his feet he said in a little louder voice than the first time, "Guilty Your Honor."

The Judge looked straight into the eyes of this bewildered and troubled individual and suggested to him, "I strongly recommend that you should get your own attorney to handle your individual case." The Judge then turned to the security guard and instructed him to take the accused, who just pleaded guilty, into custody. The Judge then stated, "This case will be handled separately."

At this point, the Judge instructed the attorney, Alfred Smith for the accused, to proceed with his opening statement. The attorney then got out of his chair, looked straight at the jury as he slowly walked up to the rail separating the jury from the rest of the court. The attorney, in a low voice, started to explain the situation that caused the government to create this new city. As his voice slowly started to get louder saying, "The accused chairman of the board and all the members of that board were charged by the authority of overseeing the entire construction of this new city. Including the hiring of all required professional people in the construction industry to design is project, as well as all the construction companies to actually build this entire new city. The project is huge and awesome. The chairman and the entire board put in a huge amount of time and energy to carry out their mandate. The responsibility and pressure that was placed upon this entire board weighed heavily on their shoulders. However, it was a responsibility that was given to them and they address the problem with an honest huge effort to carry out the creation of this entire new city." The defense attorney went on to explain all the details, problems and decisions that the board had to make to carry out the project successfully. As the attorney kept speaking, his voice slowly got louder and dramatic in an effort to sell the jury on the fact that the accused carried out their mandate of this herculean project that is now successfully providing homes and a commercial facilities that our citizens can enjoy. Then, with the dramatic swagger, walked over to the defense desk and seated himself.

It was now the prosecuting attorneys challenge to create the vision of the appointed Board of Directors and their chairman who ignored all the legal and honorable ways of carrying out their responsibility. She now continued, "They pocketed large sums of money that was meant to go into the construction of the project. Because of the shortage of money it was not possible to build a reliable and safe construction project. A huge amount of inferior substitutions of material and very substandard construction methods were built into the project. All these conditions that were shameful and built into the project, disregards the knowing fact that they created all those dangerous conditions. All these dangerous conditions affected all the residents, store owners, visitors, and the general public passing by each building on the sidewalk in front of every structure within this entire development." In making her presentation, the prosecuting attorney started out with a strong voice that got stronger as she spoke, creating the dramatic negative affect that will translate to the jury. The prosecuting attorney then took her seat.

The Judge then, addressing the attorneys for both sides of this case, gave the usual instructions and then stated, "Will the prosecuting attorney please call your first witness."

The first witness was the Secretary of the federal department of Housing and Urban Development, usually referred to the term "HUD". The Secretary then started to explain, in detail, the legislation and conditions that were approved by the Congress. He then went into a long explanation, of the detailed conditions

43

of this legislation. Continuing, he stated that the mandate required that a legal nonprofit organization shall be created. This legal nonprofit organization shall be responsible for creating and carrying out the design and construction of this entire new development located in the Bronx, a borough of New York City. He then concluded by saying, "This legislation also stated that no member or chairman of the Board of Directors of this newly created nonprofit organization, shall profit in any way beyond the stated yearly salary noted in the legislation in carrying out the requirements of their duties noted in the legislation."

The prosecuting attorney then walked over to her table and picked up a large document. She then held that document in the air, above her head, and let go of the bottom portion of the document that unfolded while holding the first page tightly in her hand between her fingers.

She then, in a very strong voice continued by saying, "This is a legal document that goes into great detail explaining all and every condition that the chairman of the board and all the board members of the nonprofit organization were mandated to follow. This document also, in great detail, outlines every mandated condition of the nonprofit organization document that the board Chairman and members blatantly violated as well as enriching themselves. By their illegal actions, they created serious dangerous conditions that were built into the construction of every building throughout this entire development."

The prosecuting attorney then stated, "This document was created and consisted of an approved committee of professional architects and engineers appointed by the District

Attorney. Each architect and engineer on this committee were not part of the original design team that created this project."

"This document outlines, in detail, all the substandard construction as well as substitution of quality equipment that was specified, with substandard inexpensive equipment with a very short lifespan."

She then turned to the Judge and said, "Your Honor, I would like to suggest that a copy of this document be put in the record and copies distributed to all members of the jury." The Judge then stated, "I will take that under advisement."

She then continued, "I will point out a few of the horrible conditions that were created and noted in this document. These items will give you a good understanding of what the entire document is legally explaining." Then she continued with her explanation of dangerous conditions that were built into the project.

She then stated, "I have listed, and submitted to the court, the names of every member of that committee, plus insurance adjusters that I intend to call to testify."

The Judge then stated that he recommends that the prosecuting attorney select one member of that investigating committee from each category of construction to save time.

The prosecuting attorney then called the structural engineer that was part of the investigating committee. A handsome young man stood up and briskly walked to the front of the court next to the table where the clerk of the court was waiting to swear him in. After the usual explanation and the response of I do, or yes, he was seated in the witness chair.

The first question that the prosecuting attorney asked was for the witness to explain what he found while going through the inspection of the buildings and how did the items of construction that he was observing compare with the construction documents. She then added, "Those contract construction documents are a legal contract for the contractor to install all material and method of installation as noted on those documents." The engineers then stated that he has a very large list of all the individual items that he observed during this inspection that was substandard and unacceptable. In addition, there were a number of items that were on the borderline of being structurally capable of supporting the load that it was designed to support. "In my opinion, all those conditions are not safe. We have a factor of safety built into every condition to make sure that there would never be a structural failure. I cannot say that the buildings as constructed has that factor of safety and therefore, in my opinion, not structurally capable of supporting the load that it was intended to support, therefore those conditions are unacceptable."

The structural engineer then went on to describe a long list of substandard construction that he was concerned with and felt that they should be reinforced or replaced. At the engineer's conclusion of his testimony, he shook his head from right to left indicating a negative body language movement and stated, "This is the worst construction project that I have ever seen in over twenty years of my professional practice as a structural engineer."

Prosecuting attorney then stated that she has no further questions. The Judge then asked the defense attorney, "Does you wish to cross examine the witness?" "No, Your Honor", he said. "Not at this time."

The Judge then said to the prosecuting attorney, "Call your next witness." He then called the heating ventilating and air conditioning engineer and asked him to describe what he found during his inspection. He started by saying, "My testimony is the same as a structural engineers except in my case it's mechanical equipment such as heating units, cooling units, pumps, fans, etc. Everything I noticed was substituted from the quality specifications that was written as part of this project. Everything that was installed that I observed was working. However, when the occupants have a very hot day, I doubt that the equipment that was installed, would be capable of cooling down the apartment efficiently. On a very cold day, I question if the installed equipment would be capable of heating up the apartment efficiently. During my complete inspection, I found that every piece of equipment that was installed was of lower grade substandard substitutions of what was called for in the specifications. This construction is shameful, extremely shameful. If you want me to describe in detail the actual conditions that I have submitted on all my documentation of this inspection I am glad to do so." The prosecuting attorney then turning to the witness and said, "That would not be necessary and thank you for your testimony." She then faced the Judge and said, "No further questions, Your Honor." The Judge then called for the defense attorney and stated, "It is your turn now. Do you want to question the witness?" "Not at this time, Your Honor."

The Judge then turned to the prosecuting attorney again and requested that she call her next witness. She then called the electrical engineer. The same procedure of being sworn in by giving the typical answer, yes I do, and was seated in the chair ready for his testimony. The prosecuting attorney then asked the same question that she asked the other engineers, and that was, "What were the conditions that you found during your investigation of all the buildings as constructed of this project?" The electrical engineer started by saying, "The biggest problem was the installation of the entire wiring system within the buildings. My drawings and specifications stated that all wiring shall be, as you know, Your Honor, the word shall is mandatory, all copper. What I found was that the entire project was installed with aluminum wiring. The big difference between copper and aluminum wiring is the coefficient of expansion and contraction. That coefficient of copper is much smaller than aluminum. Therefore, when the wire heats up they expand very slightly and when it cools down it shrinks very slightly. The result of copper is that all set screws that hold in place the copper wire, never loosened or dislodged. With aluminum, especially the main wiring coming into the building which is much thicker, the expansion and contraction is quite a bit greater when the current is running through it, and then shrinks quite a bit when it is cooling down. As a result, the aluminum wire starts loosening from the set screw and pops out. Breaking the current and shutting off all electricity to the building and equipment that is on that particular line upon the location of each condition at every connection point. I also found a major amount of equipment was a lower grade, cheaper substitution of what was specified. In my opinion, the entire electrical construction is substandard and, in my professional opinion, should be replaced."

The prosecuting attorney then continued with her examination of the plumbing engineer. His testimony was exactly the same as the other engineers, except he was speaking in terms of plumbing. The plumber's conclusion was the same, everything installed in this building was not in keeping with the drawings and specifications and therefore they were all substandard and should be replaced with the specified items.

For her next witness the prosecuting attorney called to the stand the CEO of the insurance company that supplied all the required insurance for and as directed by the Board of Directors of the nonprofit organization.

The first question that she asked the CEO of the insurance company was, "Did you receive any insurance claims from any of the tenants either in the apartments or the commercial stores of this project? Also any insurance claims from the construction companies or individual members of the construction companies, or the general public who might have been injured due to the substandard construct?" He answered with a quick "yes". Then he added, "We received claims from a number of people in all the categories that you mentioned." The CEO then continued, "However, our company has hired a group of attorneys that are now examining all the claims from the tenants, store owners, and individual citizens who was visiting tenants of the various building as well as the construction companies themselves in an effort to determine who and what is covered by the insurance. Since most of the problems in this project have to do with the substandard construction, a huge amount of questions have been raised to determine the intent of the requirements of the insurance policies that were agreed to and signed by all parties. Once the attorneys report is finalized and submitted to the insurance company Board of Directors, then we will make the determination as to how we shall proceed in the future. There isn't any more information that I have or authorized to report to the court at this time."

The Judge then asked, "What is the amount of time that your attorneys need to make a final determination, as well as the time needed for your Board of Directors to act on the information that the attorneys have supplied?" The CEO's answer was simple, "At this time, Your Honor, I do not know. However, as soon as I find out I will pass that information onto the prosecuting attorney and the court."

At this point all eyes turned to the Judge as he stated, "We shall recess this court until I receive all of the information from the attorneys and the insurance companies, and are able to make a determination as to when it would be practical to continue this case. Court dismissed."

Chapter 12

The Architect and the Secretary

William, the new and hardworking junior partner of his architectural practice, joined many "meet and greet" business network organizations. He was now meeting and creating friendships with a great many business people in various industries in the greater New York area. Through these organizations, William was able to start bringing into his office potential clients. A number of these potential clients developed into actual clients who hired William's firm as the architect for their proposed projects.

William was now very busy working as a complete involved partner of his architectural firm. Due to the additional time demands that was being put upon him, he had to hire a secretary to help him with his daily clerical duties. The name of the young secretary was Francis Gross. Francis was a bright, efficient secretary that was able to make William's working day more efficient. He now had more precious time to devote to his architectural projects for his clients. Francis was working very closely with William on a daily basis. One day about 11:30 AM, William completed his dictation of a long involved document when he turned to Francis and asked, "Will you join me for lunch?" She looked a little surprised as she quickly answered simply, "Yes."

William took Francis to a lovely Italian restaurant in the neighborhood. They spent a delightful lunch getting acquainted on a social basis and feeling very comfortable with one another.

Once lunch was finished, they went back to their office to continue the daily chores. It did not take long for both William and Francis to have lunch together every day. The discussion at one of these lunches led to William asking Francis to accompany him to a Broadway theater show that he was to entertain a client and his wife that evening. She said she would be delighted to join him and his client that evening.

The evening of the theater adventure arrived as William rang the bell at the home of his lovable secretary, Francis. She opened the door. William took a deep breath to improve his vision of this beautiful young lady, stunningly dressed, that was going to spend the evening with him and his client.

They then drove to the theater district, seated in the car waiting in line to enter the parking garage where they can leave their car for the evening.

Then, as arranged, the two couples met at an upscale, very expensive, well-known steakhouse in the theater district. The food was terrific, the two couples became friendly very quickly. They all enjoyed that great dinner getting to know each other.

Once dinner was completed, they hailed a taxi to drive them to the theater. As everyone encounters at arriving at a New York City Broadway theater, they were entertained by a young man standing at the curb of the sidewalk in front of the theater playing a saxophone. His saxophone case was open on the sidewalk at his feet and contained quite a few one dollar bills donated by people as they waited for the theater door to open. One of those persons who dropped the one dollar bill into the saxophone player's case was William. The two couples then stood in the lobby shoulder to shoulder until the theater doors opened. This also was a standard New York City theater adventure.

William was able to purchase fantastic theater seats up front and center with a clear unobstructed view of the entire stage.

The lights dimmed, the curtain opened and the show started. At the intermission, everyone then went to the rear part of the theater for two reasons. Reason one was a toilet break. And as always the men quickly entered the toilet, finish their business, came out, then reason two, went up to a makeshift counter that sold Diet Coke's at a huge inflated cost as well as hard liquor. The men with their drinks then found the seat and waited for the women who had to stand in line for quite a while until they were able to make their way into the toilet to conduct their business. Once the women were done with their business, the chimes rang notifying everyone to return to their theater seats for the second part of the show. At the conclusion of the show, another standard New York City procedure was to stop off at a cocktail lounge in the area, stand in line to get a table, and then enjoy their after theater drink. At the conclusion of that adventure, our theater goes kept hailing taxis, until finally getting one to stop and pick them up to take them back to the garage where the car was parked. Then stand in line to pay the parking fee, stand and wait for their car to be delivered, give the person who retrieved your car the standard tip, then maneuver through the N.Y. traffic, and then home. [You think life is easy in New York?]

After three months of polite dating, William and Francis were struck in the heart by Cupid's arrows. They were now officially a couple.

Chapter 13

The Trial Continues

Three months passed since the Judge declared the trial was in recess waiting for information from the CEO of the insurance company and the chairman of the Board of Directors. At last, the insurance company got their act together and requested that the Judge call the trial back into session. The Judge then sent the notice out to all participants of this trial that the trial will continue on Tuesday, the 12th of this month.

Everyone, except the Judge, was now at their seats in the courtroom waiting for the trial to be called into session. After about a short ten minute wait, everyone in the court room heard the words "Please rise".

The Judge entered the courtroom, took his seat at the high impressive desk with the fancy woodwork behind him on the wall. The Judge then said the usual, "Please be seated. The court is now in session."

The Judge then sarcastically said, "Mr. Insurance CEO, do you have information for me?" "Yes, Your Honor." The CEO then opened his briefcase and retrieved a large document, the size of which looked more like an Oxford dictionary, and handed this document to the clerk who presented it to the Judge. The first words out of the Judge's mouth was, "Are you kidding? This document contains all the insurance claims against all the buildings in this development? Are you sure you didn't mix this up with some of the other projects that you have?" "No, Your Honor. That's everything that we received from the Board of

Directors and the individual attorneys representing the various tenants, store owners and general public.

The Judge then direct his comments to the chairman of the board. "Have you reviewed every one of these claims? And are they all legitimate claims that the insurance company has to act upon?" In a low voice with his head down you could hardly hear, "Yes, Your Honor." "What percentage of the total money that you are obligated to pay that you have in the bank at this time to satisfy those claims?" Again in a low voice, "55%." The CEO then continued by saying, "Your Honor, we have a good relationship with the FBI who from time to time contacts us for information that they need on various investigations that they are conducting. Therefore, as a friendly gesture, they informed us that two of our insurance adjusters were profiting in the amount of payments that our insurance company paid to the nonprofit board. The two adjusters are no longer employed by our insurance company, and legal action has been taken against the two men."

The Judge then stated, "Your action is very commendable, and I thank your insurance company for being a responsible organization. That matter will not be part of this trial since you have everything under control."

The Judge then looked that the insurance CEO and asked, "What is the total amount of money for all those claims that were submitted to your insurance company, how much of that money are you legally obligated to pay? How much of that money is questionable? Lastly, how much of that legally obligated money does not fall within your insurance company's obligation and will be the responsibility of the nonprofit Board of Directors?" The CEO then picked up the Oxford dictionary look-alike which was the insurance report, and stated, "Your Honor, turn to page 192, you will see that chart at the bottom of the page. It indicates all the information that you requested."

1-Total amount of all claims filed with our insurance company--$76 million dollars.

2-Total insurance companies legal obligation to pay--$59 million dollars.

3-Total amount of money that the nonprofit building Board of Directors are obligated to pay--$17 million dollars.

4-Total amount of questionable claims--$5 million dollars.

The Judge then stated, "These numbers are mind boggling. I never experienced a construction that has claims in such a huge amount. What the hell was the Board of Directors doing?"

"If my math is correct,

Total claims----------------------- $76 million dollars

Insurance obligation-------------- $59 million dollars

Board of Directors obligation-- $17 million dollars

Questionable claims-------------- $5 million dollars

Total legal obligation is $76 million dollars, plus whatever the final amount comes to from the questionable claims."

"Board of Directors money on hand to satisfy claims-$2,400,000 dollars."

"That leaves $14.6 million dollars unaccounted and floating in the winds. Plus the 5 million unaccounted for claims."

At this point, the Judge stood up from his chair, looked straight at the defense and prosecuting attorneys and said, "I think I have the solution for this entire situation. I want to double check what I am thinking of to make sure it will work and satisfy both parties. At this time I would like to adjourn this session so I have the time to read this entire report and make sure that the entire situation I am thinking of will work."

"This session is now adjourned and we will meet tomorrow at 1 PM."

The prosecuting attorney reasoned that the Judge was up to something. The more she thought about it, the more she realized that something was wrong with the financing that the board of this nonprofit organization was involved in. On a hunch, she called a personal friend who worked for the FBI. She asked the friend if he was familiar with this entire investigation. "Yes, I am very familiar with all the details of our investigation into the entire mess." She then asked him if it was possible to get all the documentation of the money that was transferred from the federal government to that nonprofit organization in the South Bronx.

"Yes", her FBI friend said. "That would be no problem. Give me about one hour and I will fax you a copy of the entire documentation in reference to the flow of money from the HUD to the South Bronx nonprofit organization."

"While I have you on the phone, I have another request. I have a gut feeling that if my assumption is correct and the money that the board received went into their pockets rather than into construction, if the evidence gets too close to the Board of Directors, I can imagine them disappearing down in South America someplace to avoid any further prosecution. Can I request that the Judge should put the entire Board of Directors on house arrest under FBI supervision? This house arrest shall be enforced until this entire trial was completed so that the Judge can make a final decision in this case?" "In my opinion, the FBI agents said, yes. However, that decision would be up to the Judge."

As the prosecuting attorney went over the information, it was very clear as to the amount of money that was going into the pockets of the nonprofit organization Board of Directors. The amount of money that the board members were putting in their pockets was very much greater than the money spent on construction. There is enough information in this document for the Judge to be able to come to a decision in this case. Tomorrow is going to be an interesting day.

Chapter 14

Decision Time

The next day as court proceedings began, the prosecuting attorney addressed the Judge notifying him that she had additional information that she would like to put in the record at this time. The Judge then said, "Can I see this documentation?" "Yes, Your Honor." She then approached the bench and handed the clerk the entire package. Then the clerk handed the package to the Judge. The Judge then, looking at the document stated, "There are quite a few pages to read. Let's take a break for twenty minutes and then I will make a decision as to this new evidence. If it is relevant to this case, then I shall present a copy to the defending attorney and put this documentation in the record. Please be back here promptly in twenty minutes."

In exactly twenty minutes, the Judge was back in his seat, as were everyone else in this trial, and started the proceedings. He then requested that both attorneys approach the bench. He stated that he had the new documentation that can have a definite effect in relation to this case for both parties. "I reviewed this documentation and will allow it to be put into the record. I had my clerk make a copy of this documentation for you, Mr. Defense Attorney", as he handed the document to the attorney. The defense attorney glanced at the documentation and recognized it immediately. He felt the chill go through his body as he tried to keep his composure. The defense attorney then requested that the Judge give him two hours to review this documentation with his clients.

The Judge thought for a moment of the defense attorneys request and then said, "No I don't think you need any time because I am very sure and confident that your clients are well aware of everything that's in this document." The Judge continued, "I will give you fifteen minutes to have a quick discussion with them and then this case will proceed." The Judge then declared a fifteen minute recess for the defense attorney to speak with his client. He then hit the gavel on the block, stood up as he was saying, "See you fifteen minutes."

The fifteen minutes went by quickly and everyone was now in their places as the Judge declares that this trial is now in session.

The Judge then turned to the prosecuting attorney and said, "Counselor, are you ready to introduce and put the new evidence you discovered into the record of this trial?" She then stood up and said, "Yes, Your Honor." She then handed two additional copies of this new evidence to the clerk of the court, who then handed them to the Judge. The Judge then turned to the defense attorney, "I have an official copy of this new evidence for the record." The Judge then handed that new evidence to the clerk of the court and then handed it to the defense attorney.

The defense attorney then quickly glanced at the first couple of pages and recognized it as the evidence that was given to him previously. The defense attorney then thought to himself, "This evidence can be a disaster in his efforts to defend his clients."

The defense attorney then looked at the Judge and stated, "Your Honor, I have the feeling that you are well aware of what information is in this new evidence. It is quite lengthy and requires some in depth thinking in our effort for preparing the rest of my defense for my clients. I do not want to stretch out the amount of time needed in this case. However, I'm sure you will agree with me that I am entitled to at least one hour of time to review this new evidence with my clients. Then I will be ready to proceed with this trial."

The Judge then said, "Once more folks, we have a one hour recess to allow the defense attorney time to review this new evidence with his client. Please be back promptly in one hour."

The one hour passed rapidly and everyone was receded and ready to continue this trial.

At that time, to the shock of everyone in that court room, a smoke bomb exploded that was located as close to the jury as possible, causing panic through the entire court as everyone was quickly trying to get out of the room.

The police, FBI and Fire Department were notified immediately of this explosion and quickly took control of the entire situation. It took about three hours to clear the room of that horrible smelling smoke, and check all other parts of the court room for any additional bombs. All the government agencies now started an investigation to discover who planted this bomb. The Judge was then notified that he can continue with the trial at this time, and recommended that he rules that the court should go into recess so the authorities can do some additional investigation of the court room and surrounding area.

The Judge then quickly stated, "This court is now in recess. Since it is Thursday, and the authorities need time to investigate, this court will remain in recess until Monday morning at 9 AM."

Then, with a quick swing of his hand so that the gavel hit the tablet on the table as the Judge stood up and left the courtroom and everyone else also started to leave for the three day weekend.

Chapter 15

The Smoke Bomb Investigation

The FBI and New York City Police Department quickly started their investigations. The FBI was assigned to coordinate this entire inspection with all related government officials. The FBI then requested that the Judge keep this case in recess until the FBI is confident that no further physical attack would be attempted during the following sessions of this case. The Judge agreed and stated that this court shall remain in recess until further notice. The Judge gave instructions to the clerk of the court to make sure all parties involved in this case, as well as the general public, are advised that this court will not be in session until further notice.

A team of investigators from the FBI started to comb through the entire area of the court where the smoke bomb exploded. They were able to find a few samples of very small fragments of cardboard, metal and paper that was not completely destroyed. The FBI laboratories were then able to trace these fragments to a computer advertising and supply company, who sold strictly on a retail basis to NRA, National Rifle Association, members.

Upon further checking, the FBI was able to identify the individual who ordered that smoke bomb. The FBI also became aware that this individual ordered four smoke bombs. That means, they assumed, that three of the smoke bombs are still in his possession.

The FBI then carefully set up a SWAT team to conduct a 24 hour surveillance of the home, waiting to spot the individual either leaving or returning home. It did not take long for the young man who ordered those smoke bombs to return home.

Armed with a search warrant, the SWAT team then broke into the house and peacefully took the young man into custody. They then searched the house and found the three missing smoke bombs.

The young man, named Harold Tinne, was brought down to FBI headquarters. They notify him of his rights to an attorney and made a telephone available to him to call his family and or an attorney.

After the passing of two hours, his father and a family attorney arrived at FBI headquarters.

The young man's father and attorney were then briefed on the entire situation so everyone was aware of the facts that were known at that time. Mr. Tinne and his attorney were taken into a room with a one way viewing window adjacent to the interrogation room. They watched and listened as one of the two FBI interrogator started questioning Harold. Harold seemed very nervous and scared of the situation that he found himself in as the central figure. He was very cooperative and answered every question quickly and truthfully. Harold then told the interrogator that a few months ago, two men that he recognized as being members of the NRA, but he did not personally know them, approached him with the opportunity of making $100 in cash. All he has to do is purchase smoke bombs from that mail order company that all the members of the NRA use, for the two men. The two men told Harold that they wanted the bombs for a practical joke they were going to use to surprise a fellow member of the NRA. If they purchased the smoke bombs, then their friend might catch wise of what was happening. So that's why they wanted Harold to make the purchase for them.

Harold then told the interrogators that he did not think that anything was wrong or illegal in buying smoke bombs to play a practical joke on a friend. So he made the purchase. However, he felt that since he was making this purchase for a smoke bomb, why don't I get four smoke bombs so I can have three in my possession until the Fourth of July. Then my friends and I can have some real fun with those smoke bombs.

The FBI interrogator then asked Harold, "If you see those two men again, would you be able to recognize them and point them out to us?" "I guess so", Harold answered. Then the interrogation continued, "How often do you go to that gun club?" "About once a month when they have their meetings." "Do you see those men at the gun club meetings?" "Most of the time, not always." "Do you make every meeting?" "Yes I do", Harold answered. "If one of our FBI agents were to go to those meetings with you, as a friend who was thinking of joining the gun club, would you be able to point the two men out to us? Do you feel that you can do that without arousing any suspicion?" "Yes, that would be easy. If I do not have to talk to those men since I really don't know them, then I feel that I would have no problem." "When is the next meeting?" the interrogator asked. Harold then, feeling more comfortable, answered in a strong voice, "In two weeks."

The interrogator made arrangements to attend that meeting with Harold. At the night of the meeting, Harold and the FBI agent arrived at the meeting early and took two seats towards the rear of the room.

The room started to fill with members as Harold was watching in an effort to spot the two men in question. And all of a sudden, there they were. Harold quickly pointed the two men out to the FBI agent and sat back quietly. The FBI agent then took out his cell phone and called the FBI agents who were staked out near the entrance of the building. The FBI agent described the two men so that they can be taken into custody at the end of the meeting when they were out of the building.

The meeting was conducted in the usual manner. Everyone seemed to be having a good time and enjoying listening to the speakers, talking to their friends, and drinking Diet Coke's. I think that is what they were drinking. Who can tell if they were drinking something stronger?

At the end of the meeting, the FBI agents spotted the two men and quietly followed them to their cars. Not to cause a commotion, they quietly spoke to the two men in a low voice notifying them that they were FBI agents and want to ask them a few questions. They spoke for a few minutes, as all the members who were leaving that meeting, got into their cars and drove away. When the scene was not that crowded they then told the two men that they have a warrant to take the both of them into custody. The two men was startled by this new development and did not react fast enough to avoid the FBI agents from putting handcuffs on both of them and directed them to enter the agent's car.

At FBI headquarters, the two men were then notified of their rights for an attorney. One of the men said, "Why do you think I need an attorney? I did nothing wrong. What is this all about anyway?" The FBI agent then said, "This is just a formality that obligates me to notify you of your right to an attorney. If you feel you do not need an attorney, then that's fine with us."

Finally, after all the bureaucratic procedures, the two men were taken into an interview room for questioning. The first question that the FBI interrogator stated was, "Why did you plant that smoke bomb near the jury in that court room?" Looking very puzzled they answered, "Set a smoke bomb to explode in what courtroom? We know nothing about any smoke bomb going off in a court room." The interrogator then said, "Don't be cute. We have solid evidence that the two of you are guilty of planting that smoke bomb in that courtroom and activated it to explode. So now I ask you again, why did you do it?" Then one of the men said, "I think I'll take that attorney now." The interrogator moved the telephone up to the two men and stated, "Make your phone call." One of the men took out his cell phone and said, "I have his number listed in my cell phone because I don't memorize phone numbers. I preferred to use my own phone if that's okay with you." "No problem", the interrogated stated. "Press the call button on your cell phone and let's get started." The call was short and sweet. As he was putting his cell phone in his pocket he stated, "My attorney is not available this evening. He will be here tomorrow afternoon at 2:30." "Great", the interrogator said. "We will reconvene this interrogation tomorrow at 2:30."

The interrogator then said, "Sit tight for a minute", as he picked up the intercom telephone, said a few words and hung up. He looked at the two men and said, "Give me a few minutes and I will be all set." After a short wait, three FBI agents walked in and stated to the two men being questioned, "Gentlemen, will you please stand up and put your hands behind your back." "Why?" said one of the men that was being questioned. "So we can put the handcuffs on you." "Are we under arrest?" "No, you are just being held until your attorney gets here and the interrogator is complete. If at that time we feel that you are not guilty of any crime, you will be set free. If we find there is enough evidence that allows us to legally take you into custody, then the real arrest procedure will go into action. So for this evening, we will give you very nice sleeping accommodations with dinner this evening, breakfast and lunch tomorrow before the meeting starts at 2:30. Any other questions?" "I guess not. Let's go to dinner."

The next day at 2:30 PM, the two men in question plus there attorney was ready for the interrogator.

The first question the interrogator asked was, "Why did you set the timer and then planted that smoke bomb next to the jury in the courtroom?" "That's the instruction we received", stated one of the men. "Who gave you those instructions?" The other man then answered the question by saying, "The letter was delivered to us by a young man, dressed in normal street clothes, riding a bicycle, as we sat having lunch at the outdoor area of Starbucks." The interrogator then continued by saying, "What did the letter say, and do you still have that original letter?" The answers was, "Yes, we still have that letter back home in my desk drawer." One of the men continuing said, "The letter stated that we were highly recommended by a close friend of yours to help us carry out a practical joke. You will be paid $100 plus expenses to make a simple purchase for us. We would like you to purchase one smoke bomb from the mail order company, guns and ammunition. When you have the smoke bomb you will then call this number, 212-541-8235. You will be told that you will receive your $100 plus costs of the smoke bomb. Please deliver that bomb to a gentleman who will be waiting for you on a park bench at the Columbus Circle entrance to Central Park. Thank you very much for your help and cooperation. Signed, a friend."

"We made the delivery and received our $100 plus cost of the smoke bomb and then went home. We had no idea that the bomb would be placed to explode in a court room. We had no idea that that bomb that exploded in that court room was the one that we purchased, until we were taken into custody, I assumed, by the FBI."

At this point, the investigation was fully operable by all law enforcement. A week went by when the Judge received a letter with no return address noted anywhere on the envelope. He opened the envelope and removed a sheet of paper that had writing on it. The message was created by removing each individual letter from the artist type plastic sheet and stick it on a sheet of paper that will become the message. When all the letters are individually placed on the paper as needed, then the entire letter is completed. This letter was then sent to the Judge.

The letter read as follows: We are the people who live in the South Bronx and were informed that millions of dollars were flowing into the hands of those crooked people that formed the nonprofit organization for the purpose of rebuilding our community. That organization mandate was to build a new, modern, safe, wonderful place, for everyone in the South Bronx to live.

Instead those lowlife people that made up the nonprofit board received all that money, and did not spend it on our new home.

Instead of using the money as intended, as well as their responsibility, they put huge amounts in their dirty pockets.

In conclusion, we want all that money, every penny of the millions of dollars that was designated for our new city, to be put in our hands so we can build our new dream community by spending every penny for construction. We will not put any money at all, not even one penny, in our personal pockets. It is time for some honest people to take control of the South Bronx.

If our demands are not met, then the South Bronx will start burning all over again.

We realize that this letter will be a shock to Your Honor and the entire community. Therefore, let this message sink into everybody's minds that are involved in this effort. We will then contact you once more in the future with more details of how the transfer of money will work, and how the construction will proceed until completion.

If you want to contact us, please prepare a document with all your information, requests etc, and your decisions. Then put an ad in the NY Times wanted section saying, "Contact New Bronx." We will then contact you as to how you can contact us and we will answer any and all of your questions.

Signed, we the people.

When the Judge finished reading this letter he said to himself, "This letter is not a shock, it is an exploding volcano." Immediately, he called the FBI to notify them of the letter and schedule a meeting with law enforcement and everyone else involved.

The meeting was set for the next morning in the Mayor's office at 9 AM.

9 AM sharp, everybody was in attendance around the huge conference table in the Mayor's conference room. If you would scan the faces of everyone seated around the table you can read the body language indicating "What the hell do we do now?"

The Mayor called the meeting to order and asked the FBI to start the conversation with the work that they had done so far, what they intend to do in the future, and what they think we have to do with this group of "We the people."

The director of the FBI for this project was, Special Agent John Wilson. He started off the meeting by stating he has all his people working on this project round-the-clock. "All our computer and information experts, field force are canvassing the area, the laboratory is ready to receive any evidence that these unknown people provide."

"The big questions now is, number 1, who are "We the people"? Number 2, How do they intend to receive the money, put it in some type of banking institution, write checks for all the construction, conduct all the requirements to complete this final project? Number 3, How do they intend the stay anonymous and carry out this mission?"

The Mayor then spoke up by saying, "Agent Wilson, that is your problem as well as the other law enforcement organizations that are working with you. You must get an answer to those questions as soon as possible. This is one hell of the political shot in both eyes."

This meeting continued for about four hours with all sorts of ideas and proposals, none of which made sense. At the end of the meeting, it was agreed that we have to give the joint effort of the FBI with the New York City Police Department time to complete their investigations. "Once that is complete we will call for another meeting and take whatever action is necessary to come to an agreeable final conclusion of rebuilding the South Bronx again."

Two weeks went by and the Mayor called another meeting, to include the same people from the first meeting.

Special FBI Agent Wilson and New York City chief investigator, Mahoney, made their joint report.

"We were able to discover that there are twenty banking institutions, each located in a variety of countries around the world that deal in numbered bank accounts. These accounts hide the identity of the persons owning that account. We were only able to find out that their clients are located somewhere in the Easton area of the United States and had already opened accounts. They refuse or were unable to provide any additional information."

"That answers question number two. We have no answer to question number one and three, at this time. However, we are working on the situation and it seems that very shortly, information will start flowing in identifying "We the people"."

In concluding the meeting, the Mayor said, "Great progress to both law enforcement agencies, thank you. When other facts are coming out, I will call another meeting."

Three weeks have passed when the FBI and the New York City Police Department announced that they have some new evidence as to who "We the people" are. The meeting was called to hear this new development. Special FBI Agent Wilson then addressed all attending this meeting by saying, "We discovered a great number of legitimate nonprofit organizations that are well known to all our citizens. They are acting as the unidentified source that will be depositing the money. They will receive the money from the federal government in addition to money received by the organizations fund raising efforts and deposit into those numbered accounts in banking institutions around the world, where this type of numbered accounts is legal."

"All the money in those numbered accounts will be used for the construction of the new community in the South Bronx. No one will be given or accepting a management fee or any other fee other than that which was called for under the federal government's regulations of this project."

"The problem that we now face is that every one of those existing nonprofit organizations making those deposits into the numbered bank accounts, refused to admit that they are making those deposits. They feel that the South Bronx construction would need additional federal money for this project. What they are doing is legal. However, it does not sound legal to the general public. Therefore at this time, at those organizations request, we are keeping that list of those nonprofit organization sealed until a final decision to make those organization names public." The Judge then notified both the prosecuting and defending attorneys of the latest situation. When the Judge spoke to the prosecuting attorney notifying her of the latest situation, she immediately requested that the

Judge declare the South Bronx entire nonprofit board be put under house arrest under the FBI's supervision. She felt that the members of the board might try to leave the country rather than waiting for the possibility to be found guilty and sentenced to a prison term. The Judge agreed and said he will put that suggestion in operation the first thing the next morning.

The next morning, the Judge declared that the Board of Directors of the South Bronx project is hereby put under house arrest. In addition, he declared that the FBI shall supervise this house arrest order.

The FBI quickly went action and took every member of the South Bronx nonprofit project board into custody and organized the house arrest for each member. An electronic ankle bracelet device was attached and locked to each member. This ankle device would be monitoring their every movement. If they ever left their house while still under house arrest, they can be easily located and captured.

It did not take long for this house arrest to hit the newspapers on the front page.

The next day, while all members of the board were in house arrest, the Judge decided to hear the case of the individual board member who pleaded guilty. The Judge requested the FBI bring that member into his courtroom by one o'clock this afternoon.

Promptly at one o'clock that member of the board who pleaded guilty was in the courtroom facing the Judge.

The Judge then started the conversation by saying, "You seem to be the one honest person that was a member of the Board of

Directors. I had the opportunity of acquiring the minutes of all the meetings that were held by the board. I came across the minutes of the meeting that was held to discuss their distribution of federal funds to the board members instead of being spent as part of the construction program. The minutes made it very clear of your position on how the money is to be spent. I read the part where you express your feelings by saying, "If the board takes the money, that is illegal and immoral and I want no part of it. If the board goes through with pocketing all that money that's supposed to go to construction, I will not take one penny of that money."" The Judge then remarked that the other members mocked you and called you Mr. honest man.

"Since you pleaded guilty, and in my opinion you are not guilty, I will sentence you to time served when you were under house arrest after you pleaded, guilty." The Judge then continued, "It is a pleasure meeting you because you represent the good in mankind. In doing my job, I hear the stories of the guilty ones and very seldom do I hear people like you. I commend you for your action in standing up to the board and sticking to your morals. You are now a free man who I know will sleep nights without the worries that the rest of your board members will be facing." The board member then said, "Thank you, Your Honor. I sincerely appreciate your kind words." He then turned and left the courtroom. He went home to continue his happy life.

Chapter 16

Change of Plans

The Judge was in his office getting ready to leave for the evening when his clerk entered the room and said, "Your Honor, we just received another anonymous letter." The Judge examined the envelope and noticed there was no return address or any evidence of where the letter came from. The Judge opened the letter and began to read the contents.

"Your Honor, we have reconsidered our proposal to you in our first letter. The reason for our reconsideration is that we felt we were asking you to trust us as an unknown participant. We now think that was asking too much of you. If you did except, it would be putting too much responsibility on your shoulders. So therefore, we have a second proposal which we feel is fair and honorable. We hope, with your approval, we can rebuild the South Bronx."

"We respectfully request that you, Your Honor, take control of all the money that all members of that unethical nonprofit board have stored away in cash or personal savings accounts, stocks and bonds, or any other savings or investment institution, in addition to any other money that was or will be issued by the federal government."

"We the people will then hire a responsible construction company who will be fully charged to correct all the construction with respect to the insurance claims, and then complete the rest of the project that has not yet been constructed."

"We will then hire a legitimate supervising contractor to oversee the construction of the contractor that is actually doing the construction. These two construction companies make up the complete construction arrangements."

"We the people will then review and approve the requisition sent to us by the construction company that is doing the supervising. If we feel everything is proper then we will submit each requisition to you, Your Honor, for payment. We feel that this system is the best system to make sure that we get high quality construction from legitimate construction companies within the approved construction cost."

"After reviewing this proposal for consideration, it would be appreciated, if you would make a public announcement as to your decision. If your final decision is that you will take control of all the money and make the payments, then we will hire the construction and supervision contractors, submit their bids to you for approval, and set up the method of handling each monthly requisition."

"We look forward to becoming partners in this endeavor with you to successfully make sure that the entire South Bronx is rebuilt, is safe, and a haven for all its residents."

Sincerely, We the people.

When the Judge finished reading this letter, the only thing he was able to say is WOW.

The Judge then made a list of five Judges that are well respected and the Judges friends. He then called in his clerk and requested that he set up a meeting with these Judges so we can discuss this proposal and get a consensus of their opinions. The Judge then also asked his clerk to set up a meeting with the FBI, the prosecuting attorney, and the defense attorney.

He finished with his clerk by saying, "Let me know what you finalize as soon as possible. Now I am going home and try to rest and not think of any of this business for one night."

That evening, the Judge received a phone call from the FBI informing him that they just found out that those twenty well known nonprofit organizations canceled their account numbers with all those overseas banks. All the money was withdrawn from those accounts and were set up in a fund with a local New York City bank for safe temporary keeping.

After hearing that latest news, the Judge realized that the "We the people" second proposal is for real.

The next morning, the Judge was seated in a large conference room that was part of the courthouse, with the five Judges who were his friend to seek advice and counsel.

The Judge then went into great detail of the entire situation and the "We the people" organization proposal. After much discussion, it was agreed by all the Judges in attendance that the Judge in this case should take control of all the money, as suggested by "We the people".

The Judge then thanked his fellow Judges and stated that he will take their advice and get this project moving.

The next morning the Judge directed his clerk to put an ad in the New York Times stating, "Contract New Bronx"

Chapter 17

The Smoke Bomb, again

FBI Agent Wilson contacted the Judge to inform him that they were able to assemble all the facts in the case of who was responsible for that smoke bomb that exploded in the courtroom. Agent Wilson then said, "Your Honor, you're not going to believe this. The brains behind the entire smoke bomb was the chairman of the nonprofit board that is now under house arrest. After a long drawn out interrogation session with the chairman, he broke down and admitted that he was the one who made arrangements to hire those two young men to buy the smoke bomb. He then made arrangements for one of his people to plant the bomb in the courtroom and set the timer to explode at the time when most of the trial action was being conducted."

"We have removed the chairman from house arrest and placed him in a jail cell for safekeeping. At this time, Your Honor, he is yours."

The Judge then asked, "Did the chairman inform you what his motivation was in arranging to place that bomb and have it explode?" "Yes, Your Honor", agent Wilson said. "He felt that a physical disruption of the courts proceedings may sway your thinking, Your Honor, away from the chairman's guilt and start an action and find the person who is really the guilty one and not the chairman and members of the nonprofit board."

Agent Wilson continued, "In my opinion, that was a stupid way of thinking and action that he took."

The Judge thanked agent Wilson for the information and then sat back in his chair, and relaxed at the conclusion of that smoke bomb episode. "Now, I can concentrate fully with the case on hand and start planning the adventure with "We the people".

Chapter 18

New Partners

The Judge placed an ad in the New York Times address to, "Contract New Bronx".

The ad read as follows, "To my new partners with a clean start, success is almost guaranteed."

Three days went by since the ad was placed in the New York Times, when the phone on the Judge's desk rang. The Judge answered the phone with the usual, "Hello." The voice on the other side said, "Partner, I think it's time we got together." The Judge was startled for a few seconds as he realized who was on the phone. He then asked, "Are you ready to divulge your identity?" "Yes, Your Honor. Not only I, but all, "We the people", the entire group. We are all looking forward to meeting you face-to-face and set up a legitimate organization that will successfully rebuild the South Bronx." That voice then continued, "I don't know if you realize it, Your Honor, but right now you have become a member of "We the people." How does that sound?" The Judge replied, "Adding my new title as described sounds great. I look forward to our meeting." "Okay, the Judge continued, when and where would you like to meet?" The voice on the phone then said, "How about in my office?" "Great", the Judge said, if I knew who you were and where you are located." "Fair enough", the telephone voice said. "My name is Ronald Coleman, and I am the CEO of General Dynamics. My office is on the 14th floor of the Chrysler Building. We could meet this coming Tuesday at 9 AM. You can have your own breakfast at home if you would like, however, we take good care of our visitors and provide a very adequate display that is guaranteed to relax your entire body so you can sit back and get involved in our discussion of this meeting. How does that sound?" The Judge replied, "I cannot wait until we have that meeting. This looks like a new great adventure for me. I assume, the Judge continued, you will have all the members of "We the people", in attendance?" "Yes, Your Honor. We will all be here ready to do business." The CEO then added, "Your Honor, if you would feel more comfortable with a member of the FBI, and anyone else by your side, please feel free to bring them. They will be my guest so bring them along." The Judge said, "I'm a grown man and I can handle this all by myself. However, I will bring the FBI and both the prosecuting and defense attorneys. Thank you very much. I look forward to meeting you." Both men hung up and a new adventure was now on its way.

The Judge then quickly called the prosecuting attorney, defense attorney as well as the FBI. He requested a meeting immediately so he can explain these new exciting developments.

Two hours later, at the designated time, the Judge was waiting in the conference room for both attorneys and Agent Wilson of the FBI to arrive. Everyone was on time to this impartment meeting.

At that meeting the Judge informed every one of the telephone call with the CEO of General Dynamics. Agent Wilson said, "Wow, that's a shocker. General Dynamics is a huge worldwide corporation that is well respected were ever they set up offices, factories, and all other requirements of their business. We have some very high powered people that we are now doing business with. I can see nothing but success with this caliber of partners."

Everyone at that table agreed and was very anxious to meet the entire new group noted as "We the people". The Judge then asked everyone at the table, "Do you think it would be advisable if you would attend the meeting with me?" Agent Wilson then said, "I don't think it would hurt and besides I would love to meet our new partners." Both attorneys then said, "We second that motion. I would love to attend the meeting with you." The Judge said, "Since I was asked if I wanted to bring anyone else along, I said yes, your invite is appreciated. Remember they serve breakfast." The Judge then called his clerk and said, "Please find out for me the name of the CEO of General Dynamics, as well as his phone number. I spoke with him this morning and I didn't get that information. I guess I was too overwhelmed by the caliber of the person I was meeting with. We have a meeting set with him and all his people that are involved on Tuesday at 9 AM." The Judge then turned to his clerk and said, "When you get that CEO's name and phone number, please give to me, the defense attorney, the prosecuting attorney, and the FBI. They will be attending the meeting with the CEO on the 14th floor of the Chrysler building Tuesday at 9 AM. Thank you."

When the clerk gave the Judge the phone number of Ronald Colman, he then called the CEO and informed him that he change his mind and will be bringing three people, the prosecuting and defense attorneys as well as an FBI agent.

That Tuesday morning at 9 AM the Judge, the two attorneys and FBI agent were escorted into the conference room of General Dynamics. Seated around a huge conference table sat ten men, three women and the CEO of General Dynamics, Ronald Colman.

Ronald Coleman then stood and said, "Good morning to our new partners. Please be seated and make yourself comfortable. The breakfast wagon will be here in about three seconds. I'm sure you will survive the hunger until that time." There was a small chuckle of laughter as CEO Coleman started to make the introductions. As he introduced each of the three women and ten men, it was shocking to find out that they were all either the chairman of the board or the CEO of huge corporations with holdings around the world. As the Judge soaked in the information, he realized that this is one of the richest, most powerful business groups in this country, if not in the world. I'm sure at this time we cannot fail.

At that moment, a fantastic display of breakfast items rolled in on an expensive antique type table and placed against the wall. The coffee and tea dispensers were plugged in to the electric outlet and everything was ready. The attended then left the room as CEO Ronald Colman stated, "Before we start this meeting, I suggest we have a breakfast." He then continued, "I for one never eat breakfast at home. I really do not know why. However, I enjoy it in the office. So now you're all welcome to join me." And everyone did. While enjoying their breakfast, the small talk started with introductions and getting acquainted with one another. Once breakfast was finished, an attendant entered the room and quietly removed the table and replace it with a smaller table that contained tea and coffee that were plugged into the outlet and some goodies next to the tea and coffee carafes.

Finally, since he was the host, the meeting was called to order by CEO Coleman. He gave a short two minute explanation of the situation and what type of final action needed to be discussed. The floor was then open for general discussion. The Judge started, "I'm overwhelmed by the caliber of people in this room. I say that not to embarrass you, instead to express the confidence that I now feel knowing that the South Bronx has a real chance of becoming a reality."

The Judge continued, "All the members of the board plus the chairman of the South Bronx nonprofit organization that was given the chore of rebuilding the South Bronx, is now under house arrest and very shortly will be turned over to the jury and if found guilty, will then be sentenced which would close the case. At that point, I intend to retrieve all the illegal money that the chairman and the members of the nonprofit organization managed to steal. That will include all the cash, bank accounts, stock accounts, and any other holdings where they parked all their ill-gotten money. I know for a fact that once all the money is retrieved, it will be short of the financial requirements to continue this construction." At that time, the Judge sat down as he said, "The floor is yours ladies and gentlemen."

CEO Colman then stood and said, "Our group has previously discussed the situation and are prepared to provide all the additional money that is necessary to complete the project and obtain the best product available. We also will provide the funding that is short to satisfy all the insurance claims. Once everything is completed with this project all the inferior work will be upgraded to a high standard. All new construction will also be of very high standard and all insurance claims will be completely satisfied. At that point, the entire South Bronx project completed and turned over to the authority that will administer this entire community."

"What we have to do now is set up how we are actually going to coordinate and carry out all these mandates that I just described."

"Our last proposal was that our group will hire the construction company as well as the inspection company to make sure that all the work is completed with the highest quality of material and workmanship. We would make funds available to the Judge who will then pay all the approved requisitions. Our group as today have the ability to select construction and management companies and have the ability to monitor everything that was being constructed on the site. All the members of my organization, CEO Willoughby stated, will be doing whatever it takes to finally complete this project without any additional compensation for their time. It seems to me, the CEO continued, we do not have much to discuss. Every one of the people on my side who are attending this meeting are ready and committed themselves and their organization's and geared up to take on this challenge. Your Honor, we just have to make sure that you are ready to take on your challenge of retrieving all the money that was stolen or should I say, as much of the money that was stolen. And also make sure that we designate the legal entity that has a responsibility of completing this project."

The Judge then said, "That would be no problem. It should not take the court much longer to complete this trial and send to the jury. Once a jury makes their determination, and I assume they will find a guilty verdict, I will be able to get control of not only the money but the entire South Bronx operation. If everything goes as planned at that time, I will decimate your organization, this CEO, as the legal entity that will be completing this construction project."

One of the female CEOs then said, "Your Honor, what if the jury comes up with a verdict other than guilty?" The Judge then spoke up by saying, "I will be submitting this case to the jury broken up in cases that have to be judged. I feel confident that they will find a guilty verdict for all the sections that I will be presenting to the jury. However, in the field, some of the sections that the accused was found not guilty, then I can retrieve the money for the guilty portion and the various sections of the charges that we will be presenting to the jury. However, I am very confident that the jury will find all sections guilty. I cannot guarantee that. However, I feel that's what will happen. I suggest that we cross that bridge when we get there."

After another hour of discussion, the final details of this agreement was created and put in writing. A complete written document was then created by the attorneys CEO's Willoughby's staff for review and approval or corrections by all members present at this meeting. Copies of the final agreement were handed out for everyone's signature which was obtained very expeditiously. Everything now was finalized and this meeting is now adjourned.

Before anyone left the room there was a lot of handshakes, small talk and a good time was had when an attendant working at General Dynamics wheeled out a small rolling table with a number of bottles containing a hard drink such as Jack Daniels, etc.

Finally, everyone started to exit the room and all went on their own daily chores.

The Judge then spoke to both the prosecuting and defense attorneys and said, "The time now is to finalized this case. Are

the two of you ready to give your speech to the jury?" "Yes",
they both explain. "Great", the Judge stated. "Tomorrow is the
beginning of the final part of this trial and adventure. Have a
good day. We will see you tomorrow in court."

Chapter 19

The Summation

The prosecuting attorney rose from her seat, slowly walked to the rail separating the jury from the rest of the court. This action brought her closer to each member of the jury as possible. She started in a low calm voice by reminding them of the horrible facts and actions by the accused chairman and members of the board that were exposed during the testimony. "The accused committed those illegal and immoral acts of stealing the construction money for their own profit as well as creating dangerous life threatening living conditions. All their actions were knowingly carried out without any thought as to the dangerous affect that they are causing all the residents. Many of those residents are neighbors and friends." She continued, as her voice slowly became louder, "The accused negative illegal action by stealing the construction money and creating dangerous physical conditions that affects the safe and well-being day-to-day living of everyone residing in this community. These heartless, thoughtless, selfish, dishonest people must pay for the sins with a long term residents in a state penal institution. When you are deliberating this case, think of your children playing happily in those dangerous conditions. Can you sleep at night knowing that fact? What about the senior citizens whose health is not what it used to be and in most cases have trouble walking. Imagine them walking with a cane or some other aid such as a walker, and then due to the poor construction that created an unknown trap that will have that senior citizen fall. Once that senior citizen has fallen, walking gets much more difficult to maneuver if not completely unusable and find themselves in a wheelchair. From now on that senior citizens health is deteriorating making living much more difficult. That senior citizen can be one of your parents or even a child. How comfortable do you feel living in those conditions that the members of the board, plus the chairman deliberately, knowingly, created for personal gain? Think hard, ladies and gentlemen of the jury, of these conditions during your entire deliberation. The only conclusion that you come to would be, guilty on all charges. I sincerely thank you for your service on this jury."

The prosecuting attorney then took her seat, and started to calm down.

The Judge then called the defense attorney, "It is your turn now Mr. Attorney." Defense attorney had a different approach. Got up from his chair with a little jump, with a bright smile on his face as he approached the jury. "Ladies and gentlemen of the jury, I make my remarks sweet and simple because the situation is sweet and simple. All those horrible things that the prosecuting attorney just brought to light is not the fault of the chairman of the board or the board members. They do not physically do any construction or building of these buildings. They just make decisions that go to the contractors. Why aren't the contractors in this court being questioned at this time? I think we are looking at the wrong people. The person who actually has a hammer in his hand and drives the nails into the structure that support the building should be investigated to make sure that we have the proper person on trial. During the deliberation keep this in mind. You don't want to send the wrong person, as the prosecuting attorney stated, to a state penal institution. Please, for the sake of decency, think hard during your deliberations. I'm sure if you give what I say the proper attention, the final verdict should be not guilty on all charges. Thank you very much ladies and gentlemen of the jury. I rest my case."

The Judge then said, "Ladies and gentlemen of the jury, please follow the uniform young man into the jury room. Someone will be there to inform you of all the procedures that have to be followed and how to contact me or anyone else during you're deliberation. I thank you for your service."

"At this time this court is adjourned until a decision is reached by the jury." The Judge stood up and entered the door from the courtroom to his chambers and the waiting period was now in effect.

As all the visitors were leaving the courtroom, you can hear the conversation in reference to what the jury will decide. The most common decision by most of the spectators were, guilty on all charges. However, there were a number of people who were swayed by the defense attorney and wondered, "Maybe we should investigate the actual people who were building those structures."

It was plain to see that none of these spectators were undecided as to any decision as they left the courtroom to dinner, or a movie, or gathering in a friend's house, or even maybe going to a ball game. All the problems of the trial is now out of their heads, in fact it never was in their hands.

The prosecuting attorney and everyone who was involved in this case figured this would be a short and sweet decision by the jury with a guilty verdict. So let's not go too far because the jury will not be in session that long.

On the defense attorney side, they felt confident that they put enough doubt in the minds of the jury that might sway them to a lenient decision. In fact, they felt this is going to be for the jury, a long deliberation time.

The sun started to disappear in the horizon as the night approached and the jury was deliberating. At the proper time, the jury was taken to a secure hotel to spend the night. The next day, bright and early, the jury was back in the jury room and started the deliberation.

By the end of the day there was still no decision. Again, the jury was taken back to the hotel for the evening.

The next day, the jury was back at the conference table jury room continuing the deliberation.

The prosecuting attorney and all the people that felt that a guilty verdict is necessary, was starting to get nervous with the delay of the jury to come to a decision.

The defense attorney felt confident, with this delay, that he was able to sway the jury that might end up with the very lenient decision, or even maybe not guilty.

Another night passed, and in the morning the jury was again put in the secure bus and taken to the jury room.

The jury then deliberated for about three hours. And then, with a sigh of relief from everyone in the courtroom, the jury was then brought back into the court room. They took their seats and waited for instructions by the Judge.

The Judge then, looked straight at the jury and said, "Ladies and gentlemen of the jury, have you reached a verdict?" The chairman of the jury stood up and said, "Yes, Your Honor, we have." "Would you please hand your decision to the clerk of the court who will hand over to me." That was done and the Judge read the verdict with absolutely no facial expression that might give away the verdict.

The Judge then turned to the chairman of the jury and stated, "Would you please announce to the court your decision?" The jury chairman stood up and said, "The jury unanimously voted, guilty on all counts."

You can hear all the thoughts and whispers from everyone in the courtroom that created an eerie feeling for everyone in that courtroom.

The Judge then said, "You stated that the decision was unanimous. If that is not true with a person who feels they voted differently, please stand." There was silence in the courtroom as everyone had their eyes on the jury, and no one stood up. The verdict was guilty by everyone who was in that jury room deliberating the future of the chairman of the board and all the board members.

The Judge then thanked the jury and said they are now dismissed. He then turned to everyone in the courtroom and said, "This court is now adjourned."

The next big decision will be the sentencing of all guilty parties by the Judge. In the meantime, there was nothing else that anybody can do except go back to their normal daily life's and await the sentencing decision.

Finally, the day arrived when the Judge announced that this court will be in session for the sentencing of the guilty parties this coming Monday morning at 9 AM.

The Judge decided to make sentencing short and sweet and close this case completely. All interested parties are now in the courtroom anxiously waiting for the decision as they calmed down in their seats.

The Judge then said, "The guilty chairman and members of the board broke the law in such a horrible manner that put many people's lives in danger. This fact remained in the back of my head as I was deliberating trying to come to a conclusion as to what my final decision shall be. After wrestling with this problem for quite some time, I decided the following."

"The sentencing guidelines, as noted by the sentencing procedures and decisions of the law, notes that in this case I could decide to send all guilty parties to a proper penal institution for twenty years. However, due to the age of the chairman of the board plus all the board members, I do not think anyone of the guilty will last twenty years in confinement. Therefore, I sentence all members of the board, plus the chairman to ten years, without parole. In addition, all the money that they manage to transfer from the construction account to their own personal accounts are to be retrieved and put into a separate account under my supervision. All that money will be used to hire a new construction team, correct all the problems and insurance claims, and construct the rest of the property that was part of the original program. This case is now closed."

Chapter 20

The Judge and "We the People"

Three weeks passed since the conclusion of the trial. The jury found the chairman and members of the Board of Directors guilty. The Judge sentenced them to prison for ten years without parole. Everyone else involved with this situation decided to take a holiday. Hence the passing of three weeks.

The most pressing item at this time is turning over a 100% complete, safe, new South Bronx community, to all those who will be calling this community home.

The CEO of General Dynamics knew that this was the time to create a new organization. He then reasoned that a meeting including all the original members of "We the people", other organizations, including General Dynamics, plus individuals be established. He turned to his secretary and dictated a notice that is to be sent to every member of "We the people", inviting them to a meeting to establish this new organization. The note is to inform each member and organization, that on April 15 at 9:30 AM, the first organizational meeting is to be held in the corporate headquarters of General Dynamics on the 14th floor of the Chrysler building in New York City. It is important that every organization send a delegate to this initial organizing meeting.

He then created a large list of the names of each organization of the original, "We the people". The list also included, the CEO's of fifteen largest, and wealthiest corporations in this country, twenty-five various prestigious nonprofit organization. Each of whose mission is to raise a large sum of money in an effort to find a cure for every particular disease that affects human beings, provide housing for the homeless, and any other needs for these organization to raise money in an effort to support their cause which includes Judge Harold Fitzpatrick, Prosecuting Attorney Nancy Alloway, Defense Attorney Alfred Smith, Architect William Morris Thompson, AIA, FBI agent Lester White, and the mayor of New York City.

This committee consisting of forty-seven delegates that arrived at the corporate headquarters of General Dynamics on April 15, promptly on 9:30 AM.

As usual, there was coffee, juice, and an array of snacks for all the delegates to meet and greet each other, plus enjoy the free goodies.

After about ten minutes of greeting time, CEO Ronald Coleman requested that all participants please take a seat around this conference table. He then said, "If you did not finish your coffee and snack, you can take it with you and place it on the table. This is going to be a very civilized meeting."

CEO Coleman then stated that he will act as temporary chairman until our new organization develops a constitution and bylaws and conducts formal elections. "Are there any objections?" Everyone's head then shook indicating, in body language, no objections.

The temporary chairman started at the beginning of the proposed new South Bronx construction project. He continued by including all the information including the awarding of contracts, constructing all the building, streets and sidewalks, plus all utilities to supply this new city.

He then went on to explain the poor constructions, the corruption of the Board of Directors, the trial and verdict, and what we intend to do as a newly formed not-for-profit organization to rebuild the South Bronx with honor and dignity. Creating a safe and comfortable place for all local residents to enjoy.

The temporary chairman then stated, "The first order of business is to organize this new organization and establish a constitution and bylaws as well as voting for all offices of this new organization."

"We must form a committee to create a constitution and bylaws. If there is no objections, I will be glad to take on that position of chairman on that committee." There was a round of applause as everyone was smiling with the fact that temporary chairman Coleman took on that position. Now everyone is off the hook of being selected.

Chairman Coleman picked up the gavel, gently hit the wood block on the table and stated, "We the people" is now an official name and organization. I recommend that we keep the name "We the people" just as it is. Are we all in agreement?" Everyone now shook their heads in expressing their agreement that their name should be the permanent name of our new organization.

Chairman Coleman then announced that he was forming a committee to write the constitution and bylaws of a new organization. He then nominated five individuals who were seated around the conference table. The chairman then asked, "Are there any other suggestions for membership of this committee?" There was silence indicating approval of the constitution and bylaws committee. The chairman then stated that he will choose and set the dates to start their deliberation as soon as possible.

At this time, the chairman stated, "I would like to set an agenda to organize and finalize the procedures and decisions of the most pressing items in reference to getting the construction of the South Bronx back on schedule."

At that point, the Judge raised his hand and stated, "Mr. Chairman, I strongly suggest that we register the existence of our organization and the main purpose of our business. We have to make sure that our organization is the legal entity that is going to continue and complete the construction of the South Bronx. We must have legal authority and responsibility to take over the entire financial obligations, sign contracts and spend money as required to meet the goals that our organization has established."

The chairman, in agreement with the Judge stated, "Excellent point, Your Honor. I will have my legal staff do whatever is necessary to legally give us the authority to finish the construction of the South Bronx." The chairman then stated, "I recommend we meet once a month on the first Thursday of each month in this conference room at 10 AM. Are there any other suggestions?" Hearing none, "Then our meeting time and place has now been established."

"As soon as we have a final and approved constitution and bylaws, unless there are any other items that must be taken care of at this time, I think it is time to conclude this meeting. Any other suggestions?" Hearing none, "This meeting is now adjourned."

At this point everyone started to stand and congratulate one another for the formation of this organization to solve all the problems of the South Bronx.

Three weeks passed from the first meeting, when the temporary chairman sent out a memo and reminder of the next meeting date, time and place. In addition to the member meeting notice, each member was sent a copy of the proposed constitution and bylaws that was established by the appointed committee, a list of all future proposed candidates to join our organization, documentation of incorporation of this new organization and its goals.

Another week went by, making the time one month since the first meeting of the new organization which was called, with everyone's agreement, "We the people". That makes it time for the second meeting. After everyone arrived, had a good morning snacks and drinks, and were seated around the conference table waiting for the temporary chairman to officially open the meeting. And so he did with the flare of the gavel as it hit the wood block on the table, "This meeting will now come to order."

"The first order of business is to review and pass the new constitution and bylaws. I assume everyone received a copy of those documents that was sent out by the committee. Since I do not hear anyone speaking, that means that all the members received those documents, reviewed them, and you will be ready to vote to approve these documents as is. Unless anyone suggests some changes or additions."

"So now I ask whether any changes or additions would anyone like to discuss in reference to the approval of the new

99

constitution the bylaws?" The chairman waited a few moments and then said, "Since I do not hear any comments, I now put these documents on the floor for a vote. All in favor of adopting the constitution the bylaws as presented, please raise your hand." All the hands went up quickly to indicate a positive, yes I approve. The chairman then declared, "Approved by unanimous vote."

Organization requirements: Elected a slate of officers for this organization.

After a discussion period of nominating potential offices and discussions culminating in a vote, the following members were elected to serve as officers of this organization.

President & Chairman: Ronald Colman

Vice President: William Morris Thompson

Secretary: Sarah Honeywell

Recording Secretary: Alice Sweeney

Treasurer: Judge Harold Fitzpatrick

The first order of business is to get all those insurance claims settled to the point when we can start the corrective work of all deficient original construction.

One of the members, Sam Siegel, whose nickname was SS, stated that he was in the insurance business and felt comfortable that he can handle that entire situation. He continued by saying he will dedicate part of his staff and find a complete solution that this board will approve to closeout that matter.

The chairman then said, "Thank you very much SS. We accept your offer, unless there are other suggestions?" Hearing none, "Sam, it's all yours."

"The second order of business is to organize all the defective construction and proceed with a plan putting all the constructive work into action." Pat O'Dwyer then spoke up and stated that he has a great amount of involvement and knowledge of this type of work. He would be more than happy to be chairman of the committee. He too also stated that he can have part of his staff help organize all that work. Hire contractors who specialize in that type of construction. "I am sure they will be very reasonable with their pricing. I say this because my organization uses these contractors to do a large amount of similar work that my organization is involved in."

Chairman then thanked Mr. O'Dwyer for his proposed involvement.

"The last very large chore that we must get involved with is the completion of the entire project including all the construction that was not started as of this time. That construction includes a major part of this project. We first have to investigate and determine the entire amount of work that has to be done that was never started by the original contractors. This work has to be separate and above any of the work that is being handled by Mr. O'Dwyer and Mr. Siegel."

There was quiet in the room for a few minutes when one of their members stated, "I believe we have to do some research into different construction companies that best fits this construction. I would be glad to volunteer my services to do that research." The chairman then said, "It's yours Mrs. Webster."

The chairman then said, "Fantastic, I, or should I say we, appreciate all the voluntary work that we have just assigned to get this organization running on all cylinders."

The rest of the meeting was delegated to discuss the problem of legally separating all existing contractors from this project. "We must resolve any funds that should be returned to us or funds that we owe the contractors to finalize their involvement of work that they have successfully completed up to this time."

"Another discussion involves raising the amount of money that might be needed above the money that the old board had stolen and returned to us be used for the rest of construction. As well as any money that is still needed do this construction project by the federal government.

It was finally agreed that any funding discussion at this time will not be fruitful due to the lack of financing and funding requirements needed to complete the project. "Until we have the hard numbers as to how much money we will receive that was already designated for this project, and how much money we will need to finish all the work as required, this discussion will be on hold."

The chairman then looked at his watch and said, "My goodness, time does fly. Lunch time has just arrived." The chairman then asked, "Does anyone have any additional information or suggestions for further discussion?" There was silence for a few moments. The chairman then said, "Thank you very much ladies and gentlemen. This meeting is now adjourned for the purpose of having lunch and then returning at 1 PM. Just for your information, the next meeting will be next month from today, on the 1st Thursday at 10 AM. A notice will be sent out."

At 1 PM, all members returned from lunch and were seated around the conference table ready to start the afternoon session.

"The first order of business, and the last item that we have to discuss, is, fundraising. I am sure, the chairman stated, that all the money that we will be receiving from the money that was illegally taken by the old board, plus any additional funds to this project from the federal government, will not be enough to cover all the new construction work plus correcting the new unacceptable substandard poor construction, as well as the work that was never finished and still has to be done. Therefore, a major fund raising drive has to get underway."

The chairman then suggested, "As a starting point to our fund-raising effort, I will donate $10,000." He then continued, "No one is obligated to make a starting donation to our fund-raising campaign." At that time Sam Siegel stated, "I too will donate $10,000." That started the action going as each member in turn donated $10,000. And then before the end of the meeting all 40 members of "We the people", each donated $10,000 for a grand total of $400,000. The chairman then said, "Thank you ladies and gentlemen that is a fantastic start to the campaign."

"Does anyone want to start off this meeting with suggestions?" "Yes I would", stated Alex Winston. "I am deeply involved in all phases of politics from setting up election campaigns to running an office by an elected official. I have been involved in and with politics since I was a young man. Due to my age at that time, I joined the "Young Democrats". As you can see, the way I look now, I am no longer young, but just a Democrat."

"It is a known fact that on all levels of government, from the federal level to the state level and down to individual county level, all elected officials receive what is called, "discretionary funds". This money is given to the elected official to spend basically on community projects that are run by citizen groups in his or her election district. The purpose of this giveaway money is to provide legitimate community projects that is needed by the community. In addition, it helps to make friends with those community groups so that upon reelection time, you have friends out there that will vote to keep you in office. If you agree with this process or not is immaterial because it is a fact of life that has been going on for many years and by the way, it is completely legal."

"I recommend that all members of this organization who have friends or relatives who are elected officials, talk to them about discretionary funds. With the proper announcements that an elected official donated money to build a necessary item in a community, that is always good news for the elected official."

The chairman then stated, "That's good to know. Let's take that under advisement for future discussion."

Another member stated, "My organization knows how individuals donate money to various choices. We have the list broken down to people who donate to many organizations, people who are very selective in their donations, and people who do not believe in donating anything. We save a lot of money on printing and mailing costs to just send letters requesting donations to the proper people."

This type of thinking went on for quite some time until the chairman stated, "I hereby form a committee, create a complete fund raising effort that we can put into action." He then suggested the names who he felt would fit very well on this committee. All the individuals that the chairman suggested for this committee agreed to serve. The committee was now official.

The chairman then stated, "We are now all organized and ready to get into action and start producing not only money but the new South Bronx community. This meeting is now adjourned."

By the time of the next meeting, all the committees were working full blast and showing signs of accomplishment. Insurance claims were being settled, substandard construction was being catalogued and soon will begin the corrective construction phase of this portion of the work. New construction was now being organized by surveying the various neighborhoods checking all conditions and making sure all the construction drawings are complete and up-to-date to meet all the new requirements. This new construction is getting ready to start the reconstruction phase within the next three weeks.

All members of the community are excited at the progress that they are witnessing on a daily basis. In addition, those community members witnessing this new effort were feeling very good knowing that the people involved in correcting all the ills of the previous organization, are on their side.

Politicians from Washington and Albany are constantly visiting the site and viewing the fantastic progress that is being made. In addition, the entire, "We the people" organization are watching to make sure the progress stays on a positive honest footing.

As time went on with the corrective construction as well as the new construction that was on full blast, officials started to announce the completion of sections that are ready for occupancy. Residence then started to move in to those new spaces as they became available. The joy on the faces of those new tenants told the story of what they were seeing and knowing his real, safe, and a real home.

Finally, the time came when all construction was 100% complete and the community was now turned over to the legal local government and the people to enjoy.

A number of federal agencies were now studying the entire South Bronx from, the South Bronx is burning, to the South Bronx is shining. The American Institute of architects also started to study the original, horrible attempt and the fantastic and honest final phases of this created new community. A number of books will be written about this adventure as well as Hollywood poking around the entire area and creating all sorts of movies.

Chapter 21

All the New Home Owner Associations

The entire South Bronx was now one large community divided up into ten different sub communities. Each sub community established their own Homeowners Association. These ten different groups work in combination with each other for the good of all. They all had many meetings and programs that each community now thrives. There was something for everyone. The kids had their playgrounds and plenty of safe areas throughout the entire development. The parents had many programs for them to enjoy. And finally, the senior citizens were able to enjoy life with one another in their golden years.

Finally, all ten Homeowner Associations got together to plan one huge fantastic party that will be recognized worldwide. And so they did. It took a lot of hard work and quite some time before they had all put together. The joyous event was like a Mardi Gras, Fourth of July, and full blast that lasted three full days. The busiest attraction was a number of hot air balloons that would take participants up in the air so they can see the entire development as the birds do. This view was simply fantastic. A number of professional photographers, both still and video, documented the entire proceedings and created a number of fine books for keeping this magnificent creation alive forever.

The Bronx is Burning!

No,

The Bronx is Shining!

This is the end of the book and the start of the new South Bronx.

Made in the USA
San Bernardino,
CA